"Who Cares Wins":
The Art and Science of
Crisis Negotiation

Hong Kong Police Negotiators'
Crisis Interventions - An Eight-Cs Model
Embracing Passion, Nobility and Commitment (PNC)

Connie Lee Hamelin and Gilbert Wong

ISBN: 978-1-3879-2287-1 (sc)
ISBN: 978-1-3879-2286-4 (hc)
ISBN: 978-1-3879-2284-0 (e)

Library of Congress Control Number: 2021920308

Because of the dynamic nature of the Internet, any web addresses or links contained in this book may have changed since publication and may no longer be valid. The views expressed in this work are solely those of the author and do not necessarily reflect the views of the publisher, and the publisher hereby disclaims any responsibility for them.

Lulu Publishing Services rev. date: 03/01/2022

Contents

Karma Castilho, the creator of the painting on the book cover, despite having experienced a day of considerable challenge, was imbued with a subconscious desire to express her interpretation of the events that transpired on that day—a creative journey. She expressed her life weariness by dabbing, in a circular motion, sombre colours onto a canvas. Gradually, as she circled inwards, she applied brighter colours, an expression of an emerging and strengthening light beam within her core. The randomly applied, shadowy, white patches and lines simulated the light beams penetrating through the darkness.

Karma's discourse is truly profound: amidst the storm of tumultuous events in our lives, should we choose to recognise and utilise it, each of us has a safe, positive, and life-affirming place within our psyches. This powerful recognition enables you to see positivity and possibilities in events in the external world, which seem dark and intimidating.

———————◆———————

The heart of man is very much like the sea, it has its storms, it has its tides and in its depths it has its pearls too.

—Vincent Van Gogh

To all the crisis negotiators of the Police Negotiation Cadre of the Hong Kong Police Force who have helped and will continue to help the distressed souls who come into your orbit.

To the people who, through the guidance of the crisis negotiators, have heeded their own voices and taken the brave step to embrace life anew.

仁者不憂

Who Cares Wins

Motto of the Police Negotiation Cadre
Hong Kong Police Force

Crisis Negotiators' Declaration

Where there is a crisis,
Let us negotiate to bring resolution;
Where there are suicidal persons,
Let us negotiate to bring hope;
Where hostages have been taken,
Let us negotiate to bring safety;
Where kidnappings are reported,
Let us negotiate to bring rescue;
Where there is terror,
Let us negotiate to bring peace;
In our negotiations:
Let us listen and talk less.
Let us communicate and not command.
Let us understand and not judge.
Let us care and not overbear.
For it is:
With care we learn compassion.
With compassion we learn empathy.
With empathy we build rapport.
With rapport we establish trust.
With trust we resolve conflict.
It is in crisis we make a difference.
Let us make 'Who Cares Wins' a motto for everyone.

Gilbert Wong

Disclaimer

The stories in the book are based on true accounts which the police negotiators voluntarily shared with the authors. The crisis negotiators who handled the incidents have all vetted the respective scripts and have agreed to the information mentioned. The purpose of publication is for experience sharing, as a source of reference and inspiration with like-minded professionals. Therefore, it is not meant to be an authority in the field of crisis negotiation or suicide prevention.

The publisher and the authors herein and hereby hold no responsibility and disclaim liability for any inaccuracies, errors or omissions in the contents of the stories and in the field of crisis negotiation, whether such inaccuracies, errors or omissions result from negligence, accident or any other cause.

List of Images

Foreword

I am indebted to all members of the Police Negotiation Cadre (PNC) of the Hong Kong Police for two reasons. First, I had worked closely with them when I was the commissioner of police, commanding the police operations for the Sixth Ministerial Conference of the World Trade Organization in Hong Kong in 2005. I was deeply impressed by their professionalism and devotion to their task, which in no small measure led to the success of the operations. Second, I became a voluntary training coordinator after my retirement, and I frequently invited PNC members to lecture in some of my programmes. They never fell short of my expectations.

Members of the PNC are carefully selected, intensively trained, and highly motivated. The cadre requires all members to undergo an "ASK" training model, through which they learn and acquire caring attitude, practical skills, and professional knowledge. PNC members work in teams on a twenty-four-hour call-out system, efficiently supporting their frontline colleagues in crisis negotiation. In Hong Kong, the cadre is one of the most deployed police secondary duty units. As volunteers, PNC members take pride in their role but prefer to stay away from the limelight. Although the work of PNC has been positively featured in many local TV series and movies, a book dedicated to the cadre is lacking.

The two authors of this book are Gilbert and Connie. Gilbert, whom I have known for more than twenty years, is a veteran negotiator and is now commanding the PNC. He has shared his experience in several incidents that he personally handled as a negotiator. He also coordinated the sharing of other negotiators. Connie, a retired chief inspector with some experience in crisis negotiation, has preferred to put pen to paper to succinctly write up the interviews with all the contributors. Each of the thirty-four incidents mentioned in this book has its uniqueness and challenge, but not every one was resolved. In some "fallen" cases, the effort of everybody eventually came to grief, and the negotiators and their teams had to find their way out from distress.

The publication of this book marks the forty-fifth anniversary of the PNC. It is a non-fiction police storybook. It does not give you flying bullets or high-speed car chases, but you may find the blood, sweat, and tears of the PNC negotiators have stained your fingers as you turn the pages.

Dick Ming Kwai Lee, GBS, QPM, CPM
Former Commissioner of Police (2003–2007)
Hong Kong Police Force

Foreword

The year 2020 marks the forty-fifth anniversary of the Police Negotiation Cadre (PNC). The PNC came into being in 1975 under the impact of global and local safety concern at the time. Through the years, the charter of the PNC has proliferated substantially from being simply a counterterrorism unit to include the handling of barricade incidents, attempted suicide, and even public order–related incidents.

For the past forty-five years, the cadre has readily taken on the ever-changing challenges stemming from the added responsibilities and the sophisticated environment, continuing to save lives and offer a peaceful resolution to any crisis situation. Members of the PNC have always dutifully accomplished their mission and gained public confidence throughout the years, although operating in the form of a volunteer secondary duty.

To equip the cadre's readiness for the emerging challenges stemming from the evolving environment, a robust training and research protocol has been developed to enhance the professionalism of the cadre members. As one of the earliest police negotiation cadres in the world, the PNC's works and its negotiation training are world-renowned and the envy of many neighbouring law enforcement counterparts and international crisis negotiation communities.

The significant progress of the PNC can be attributed to the many challenges, big and small, faced by the force and Hong Kong. All the PNC callout cases and related photographs in this book are strong testament to the PNC's commitment to making Hong Kong one of the safest and most stable societies in the world.

I am extremely proud that over the four decades, the men and women of the PNC have lived up their motto, 'Who Cares Wins', and saved not only lives but also the souls of many. 'With faith, we go farther.' I am confident that their faith will continue to lead them to fulfil their sacred mission: to serve the people of Hong Kong.

Lastly, on a personal note, the birth of this book gives me a precious opportunity to revisit the proud history and development of the PNC and rekindle the fond memories of the good old days shared by Gilbert, Connie, and myself. Gilbert is my old comrade, and we came to know each other when we were junior inspectors working in the Kowloon West Region. Connie and I spent years together in the Criminal Intelligence Bureau. This publication is a testament to the great resolution of the police officers dedicated to the negotiation field. It is also a great reward for my old friends who unselfishly edited this book out of their love for the job, and they have every reason to be proud of their achievements.

Chris Ping Keung Tang, PDSM
Former Commissioner of Police (November 2019 to June 2021)
Hong Kong Police Force

Secretary for Security
Hong Kong Special Administrative Region, China (June 2021-)

Authors' Note

We ask the reader to respect the writing style utilised in the principal text in particular. We want the reader to really feel the immediacy of the scenes described and the raw emotions that are on display, on the parts of those attempting suicide and those people who are wholeheartedly trying to save lives. It is almost a truism to say that in the process of negotiation, there are many exchanges of conversation. We believe that the sustained use of dialogue brings the reader closer to the reality of what is transpiring.

It is impossible for the negotiators to recall all the exact dialogues. The crisis negotiators provided us with gist of the dialogues in Cantonese. In order to ensure the continuity of the storyline, we have taken the liberty of filling in any gaps in the verbal exchanges which took place. In a few cases, the negotiators could recall exact dialogue. However, the translation from Cantonese to English cannot be verbatim. Cantonese is a spoken dialect; it has to be modified and polished when converted to a writing style. There are also the grammatical constraints; for instance, in chapter 17, 'A Burglar Needs a Platform to Surrender', the verbatim Cantonese of the burglar's requests is, 'Could you not arrest me? Could you not prosecute me? Could you not bash me?' These expressions have to be modified so they are in accord with English language syntax.

The identities of the subject persons are not revealed. To protect their identities, only the year, and perhaps the season, are provided for most cases, though some have no time frame. Two cases are the exception: the negotiations with a plane hijacker and a murderer are so unique that it is pointless to hide the dates.

Preface

When people engage in self-harm, they are in states of crises and lose their ability to find coping strategies to solve their problems. At times, such cases are reported to the police. In the Hong Kong scenarios, procedures are in place for attending police officers to request the Police Negotiation Cadre (PNC) to attend the scene and assist in defusing the particular crisis. This book is about the skilled and powerful interventions of police negotiators who engage with distraught persons to persuade them to abort their self-harm attempts. The scenarios encompass attempted suicide, barricading, and hostage taking. Through face-to-face interviews, the police negotiators shared their stories with me.

I have chosen thirty-two PNC stories to be included in the book. As a highly experienced PNC commander, Gilbert has contributed a number of stories that he personally handled. There are two more stories. Dr Gregory M. Vecchi shared an attempted suicide case he handled that occurred in the United States. Greg was a former supervisory special agent of the Federal Bureau of Investigation (FBI) in crisis and hostage-taking negotiation. I included an attempted suicide incident that I personally handled during my police career. I am not a member of the cadre.

Gilbert has provided the relevant authoritative materials about the PNC in chapter one and two. On the other hand, Calvin Cheung, chief training officer of the PNC has provided information regarding the structure of the cadre; recruitment and training; operational mechanism in a crisis scenario and equipment. Along my writing journey, Gilbert has methodically read and vetted all the contents to ensure that the information in the book contains no sensitive information that might violate the disclosure policy of the Hong Kong Police Force. He ensures that the material is not only factually accurate but is also imbued with the altruism and self-sacrifice which are signifiers of the nobility and selflessness of those negotiators, who are so dedicated to the preservation of human life.

All the police negotiators have agreed to use their real names in the book. Gilbert and I had discussed the appropriateness of mentioning their names in the stories. Having considered that the stories are followed up with personal reflections from the negotiators, we feel that mentioning their names will enhance the authenticity and authority of the book. The use of personal names also draws the reader's attention to the fact that the negotiators are real people who try and uphold the sanctity of human life, irrespective of the backgrounds of those contemplating suicide and often under conditions whereby they may expose themselves to harm.

With respect to body matter, Gilbert and I discussed several options with respect to the arrangement of the case scenarios explored in this book—for example, arrangement by types of incidents, alphabetical order of the negotiators' name, or year of occurrence. Eventually, we have decided to group the narratives under Gilbert's 'Eight Cs' model. Over the years, he has developed and conceptualised eight stages to describe and explain those elements which are pivotal in the achievement of positive outcomes in the process of negotiation. The eight Cs are cordon, command, communication, control of emotion, co-ordination of intelligence, care, commitment, and closure. These concepts are discussed in more detail in chapter two.

To further add to the authoritativeness of this book, Gilbert has enlisted the support of two prominent and influential figures in the field of suicide and its prevention. I am greatly honoured to have a chance to interview Dr Paul Wong and Dr Gregory M. Vecchi.

Dr Paul Wong, Doctor of Psychology (Clinical), wears many hats at the University of Hong Kong. He has long had a keen clinical interest in research into suicide prevention and intervention for many years.

In particular, Paul has been involved in several large-scale suicide prevention research projects. He is involved in several studies, namely 'Understanding Aborted Suicide Attempts: A Mixed-Methods Study' and 'The Psychological Autopsy of Youth and Adult Suicides in Hong Kong'. He is engaged in community-based suicide prevention programmes on Cheung Chau Island and several other districts in Hong Kong. He is now an honorary research fellow of the Hong Kong Police College.

Paul has studied suicide bereavement and provided consultation to people bereaved by suicide. Recently, he has expanded his research areas and is now focusing on social inclusion of disadvantaged groups in Hong Kong, including people with mental health issues, ethnic minorities, vulnerable youths (particularly those with prolonged social withdrawal behaviour), and non-human animals (especially mixed breed or mongrel dogs). He has kindly written an introduction for this book.

Gregory M. Vecchi, PhD, retired from the FBI in February 2014 after twenty-nine years of combined service in the military and as a federal agent. During his career, Greg investigated Russian organised crime, international drug trafficking, international and domestic terrorism, and violent crime. He was formerly the chief of the FBI's legendary Behavioral Science Unit and a career hostage negotiator. After retirement, Greg served as a reserve deputy sheriff with the Buchanan and Clinton County, Missouri, Sheriff's Department.

Greg is a professor of criminal justice and homeland security at Keiser University. He conducts police training in de-escalation and use of force. Greg is an expert witness and consults in the areas of behavioural analysis, confirmation bias, crisis negotiation, interviewing and interrogation, police procedures, threat assessment, and use-of-force matters.

In the real-life story that Greg shared in this book (chapter nineteen), he illustrated the application of his behavioural influence stairway model (BISM; Vecchi et al. 2019, 230–39).

In his interview with me, Greg talked about the significant differences between the United States and Hong Kong, with respect to how crisis negotiations were conducted. His explanations, in terms of prevailing cultural dynamics, were fascinating and thought-provoking.

The hypno-paintings in the book, including the book cover, are a generous contribution from Karma Castilho, a long-time friend and clinical hypnotherapy student of Gilbert. Karma learned about our book project in June 2019. She is most supportive of our course and has agreed to contribute a selection of her paintings to enrich the written component of the book.

Karma started her painting journey in her mid-thirties. As a self-learned artist in acrylic painting on canvas, she enjoys exploring and creating different visual effects by using common materials such as kitchen tissue paper and other ordinary household items. Some of her paintings have achieved recognition awards in an international online art competition, Light, Space and Time Art Gallery. This is an artistic platform that attracts entries from highly talented painters all over the world. For more information regarding Karma Castilho's paintiSngs, please visit her website, www.gallerykarma.com.

The year 2020 marked the forty-fifth anniversary of the PNC. This book bears witness to the sustained dedication and practice of the unit's core values (passion, nobility, and commitment). Let PNC's motto, 'Who Cares Wins', be a blessing to all.

Connie

Acknowledgements

We are greatly indebted to all the police negotiators who put their faith and trust in us by sharing their stories. They are Arie Chan, Calvin Cheung, Chi Kwong Wong, Elizabeth Ma, Edwin Lui, Ken Fung, Natalie Lam, Rachel Hui, Rebecca Pang, Ricky Tsang, Sindy Chan, Stephen Liauw, Steve Li, and Wilbut Chan. The names are presented in alphabetical order of their Christian names.

We would like to thank Dr Gregory M. Vecchi and Dr Paul Wai Ching Wong for their exclusive interview with Connie and their invaluable support to the production of the book.

In addition, Paul introduces us to Dr Terry Bell, an exceptionally learned scholar and editor, holding eight master's degrees. Dr Bell first edited our book. He provided valuable critiques and refined ideas and syntaxes while keeping to the central themes. He typically provided replies within days. Moreover, he contributed all of his payment towards the cost of sponsoring five Australian children through the Smith family and supporting orphanages for children with AIDS in both Cambodia and Vietnam. Our special thanks to you, Dr Bell.

We are sincerely grateful to Mr Dick Ming Kwai, Lee, former commissioner of the Hong Kong police force, and Mr Chris Ping Keung, Tang, Secretary for Secretary of the Hong Kong Special Administrative Region for each contributing a foreword for this book. Mr Tang wrote the foreword in his capacity as commissioner of police of the Hong Kong police force at the time.

We are very thankful to Karma Castilho, who has enriched this book with her hypno-paintings.

Our special thanks to Wai-sing Chan for taking photographs to match appropriate scenarios, as well as the police officers who have assisted in the photographic casts.

We like to thank the *Sing Tao Daily Hong Kong* for permitting us to include two of their copyrighted photographs in the book. The photographs in chapter nine were taken by their reporters on the date of the incident.

Connie thanks Carol Dyer for first editing and publishing the incident of 'The Point of a Gun' in *Imprint* 18, the Annual Anthology of the Women in Publishing Society, Hong Kong (2019). This case is now included in chapter six of this book.

Connie is thankful to Dr Gillian Bickley for her inspiration and advice at the initial stage of writing the book. She attended a short course on writing life stories in December 2018, taught by Dr Bickley at the Hong Kong university school of professional and continuing education (HKU SPACE).

Connie thanks her husband, Denis Hamelin, for his unwavering support and encouragement in enabling her to pursue and fulfil her dream of becoming a writer.

Gilbert is indebted to Dr David Ka Sing Ng, Mr Tony Chi Hung Wong, and Mr Raymond Chak Yee Siu for their inspiration, and unfailing guidance throughout his twenty-eight years of service in the Hong Kong police force.

Gilbert expresses his gratitude to his wife, Sandra, for her love, care and patience. Her unconditional love has changed Gilbert's world and turned him into a better person.

Last but not least, Connie and Gilbert are so grateful to their long-time friend and colleague, Angus Pullinger, for editing several areas in the book including the back cover and about the authors.

Introduction

Incidence and Nature of Suicide in Hong Kong

Epidemiology of suicide in Hong Kong

The situation of suicide in Hong Kong appears to have improved in the past decade. News reports on suicide can still be read in local newspapers every day, not to mention those cases in which people killed their loved ones and then took their own lives (murder-suicides). Suicide is not only a public health and social issue. It is also a philosophical issue, one which creates a profound sense of unease and challenges our most deeply held belief: all human life is sacred. The suicide of another person forces us to question the value and meaning not only of life in general but also of our own individual lives.

According to the World Health Organization's world suicide report, 'Preventing Suicide: A Global Imperative' published in 2014, it was estimated that 804,000 suicide deaths occurred worldwide in 2012, representing an annual global age-standardized suicide rate of 11.4 per 100,000 population (15.0 for males and 8.0 for females). However, because suicide is a sensitive issue and is even illegal in some countries, it is very likely that it is under-reported. Suicide does not occur solely in high-income countries; it is a global phenomenon in all regions of the world. In fact, over 79 per cent of global suicides occurred in low- and middle-income countries in 2016.

Suicide in Hong Kong resulted in 853 deaths in 2016 (11.5 per 100,000). It is estimated that more than seven thousand people make non-fatal suicide attempts annually (see figure 1). In general, the suicide rate peaked in 2003 and has come down since and remained relatively stable in the past ten years. Most recent statistics show that suicide is the leading cause of death amongst fifteen- to twenty-four-year-olds, and suicide rate is the highest amongst people aged sixty or above (24.3 per 100,000 in 2017). Given the fact that our society is ageing rapidly and that there is a consequent increase in population of the elderly, it is a disturbing thought to contemplate that the suicide phenomenon amongst the elderly in Hong Kong may will, in all probability, become worse in the years to come.

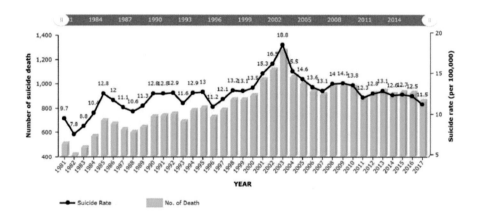

Suicide figures in Hong Kong from 1981 to 2017. Source: The Centre for Suicide Research and Prevention, the University of Hong Kong.

Who are at risk of completing and attempting suicide?

The link between suicide and mental disorders (in particular depression and alcohol use disorders) is well established in high-income countries, but many suicides happen impulsively in moments of crisis with a breakdown in the ability to deal with life stresses, such as financial problems, relationship break-up, or chronic pain and illness. Suicide rates are also high amongst vulnerable groups who experience discrimination, such as refugees and migrants; indigenous peoples; lesbian, gay, bisexual, transgender, and intersex (LGBTI) persons; and prisoners. By far the strongest risk factor for suicide is a previous suicide attempt.

In a review by the World Health Organization, several risk factors act cumulatively to increase a person's vulnerability to suicidal behaviour. Risk factors associated with the health system and society at large include difficulties in accessing health care and in receiving the care needed, easy availability of the means for suicide, inappropriate media reporting that sensationalises suicide and increases the risk of 'copycat' suicides, stigma against people who seek help for suicidal behaviours, or for mental health and substance abuse problems. Risks linked to the community and relationships include war and disaster, stresses of acculturation (such as amongst indigenous peoples or displaced persons), discrimination, a sense of isolation, abuse, violence, and conflictual relationships. Risk factors at the individual level include previous suicide attempts, mental disorders, harmful use of alcohol, financial loss, chronic pain, and a family history of suicide.

In Hong Kong, the risk factors for suicide are similar with what are being reported internationally. In 2003–2006, I participated in one of the earliest psychological autopsy studies in this region. Using a case-control psychological autopsy method, 150 suicide deceased were compared with 150 living controls matched by age and gender. Semi-structured interviews were conducted with the next-of-kin of the subjects. Data were collected on a wide range of potential risk and protective factors, including demographic, life event, and clinical and psychological variables. The relative contribution of these factors towards suicide was examined in a multiple logistic regression model. We found that six factors were found to significantly and independently contribute to suicide in Hong Kong: unemployment, indebtedness, being single, lack of social support, psychiatric illness, and history of past attempts. It was concluded that both psychosocial and clinical factors are important in suicides in Hong Kong. They seem to have mediated suicide risk independently. In addition, socioeconomic adversities seem to have played a relatively important role in the increasing suicide rate in Hong Kong.

World views on suicide in history

Most, but not all, societies and religious traditions ban suicide. For example, in the West, Socrates (469–399 BC) expressed the notion that suicide was always wrong because it represents the release of ourselves (i.e., our souls) from a 'guard-post' (i.e., our bodies) the gods have placed us in as a form of punishment (Phaedo 61b–62c.). St Augustine (AD 354–430), from a religious perspective, argued that suicide challenges the fifth commandment of the Bible, 'Thou shalt not kill.' From an alternative point of view, some Asian traditions sanction suicide under certain circumstances; for example, the practice of martyrdom in some Islamic sects, in war against an enemy, (especially if that war is constructed and defined in religious terms), suicide deaths of widowed women in Hinduism in India, and homicide-suicide as a culturally acceptable response to disgrace and dishonour.

Suicide in traditional Chinese culture was often perceived as a positive act and was actually encouraged by the state. To illustrate, Qu Yuen (屈原) committed suicide by drowning himself when the emperor refused to heed his advice. Interestingly, his death is still much respected because it is believed that his suicidal act was an act of protest, an assertion that the voice of general society should be heard by the emperor. Also, two legendary Chinese romantic musicals, *Butterfly Lovers* (梁祝) and *Princess of Cheung Ping* (帝女花), glorified suicide as a response to thwarted or unrealised love. Yet, a conflicting viewpoint is expressed in Chinese folk-belief, based on the notion of reincarnation probably rooted from the buddhism perspective.

This viewpoint holds that those who committed suicide are not allowed to get back to the reincarnation chain, are locked in the bottom level of hell, and be tortured eternally.

Modern perspectives with respect to suicide

Despite the long history of suicide in both Western and non-Western societies, it has only been in the last few decades that significant scientific study on suicide and suicidal behaviour has emerged. In these few decades, suicide prevention researchers and practitioners from medical, psychiatric, psychological, sociological, neurological, and public health perspectives have tried to understand and prevent suicide.

In particular, two schools of thought have provided the foundation for the present-day study of suicide: Emile Durkheim's sociological theory and Sigmund Freud's psychoanalytical theory. Durkheim (1897/1951) purported that suicide was an index of societal well-being and that suicide could be divided into four categories based on individual motivation and the balance of power of individual and society: egoistic, altruistic, anomic, and fatalistic. Freud (1957) suggested that personal psychological conflict, related to individual history, is responsible for all suicide.

Suicide is now perceived as a multifaceted public health problem. Edwin Shneidman, a well-respected suicidologist, noted that suicide involves overlapping domains, including biology, family history and genetics, personality traits, psychiatric disorder, psychosocial, life events, and chronic medical illness. This approach has shifted the focus of preventing suicide from purely a societal or psychiatric perspective to a biopsychosocial perspective. The major benefit of this model is the fact that it provides an opportunity to organise currently available knowledge in such a way that preventing suicide requires multidisciplinary efforts across different phases of a suicidal process.

What about its impact on families and those around?

Before discussing the subject of preventing suicide, it is important to foreground those other than the people at risk of suicide, who are the most severely impacted by suicide. Suicides rarely occur in an interpersonal vacuum. It creates tragic consequences for those who are left behind and whose lives are forever changed. Typically, people bereaved by suicide are family members, friends, and co-workers of the deceased. Nevertheless, others who may not have even known the deceased personally can also be profoundly affected by a suicide. For instances, police officers and firefighters—individuals who have attempted to save a suicidal life or have found the body of the suicide victim—may be severely impacted. In our society, a negative social label has always been attached to people bereaved by suicide. They are often explicitly or implicitly blamed for the death. Such social perceptions are unfair, are deeply wounding, and can potentially generate tremendously destructive shame in those who are already deeply grieved and guilt-ridden. Indeed, these individuals may gradually develop pathological bereavement and become suicidal themselves. It is generally said that time heals, as mentioned in a wonderful book *Night Falls Fast: Understanding Suicide* by Kay Redfield Jamison, a psychiatrist who has attempted suicide. Suicide makes a half-stitched scar on people bereaved by suicide, and the scars can be broken again and again, especially on special days like anniversaries and holidays.

What can we do to prevent these deaths?

In recent years, increasing and widespread concern about suicide as a public health problem has generated a dramatic increase in the volume of research about the causes and risk factors for suicidal behaviour. Accordingly, in 1996, the United Nations published guidelines to assist and stimulate countries to develop national strategies aimed at reducing morbidity, mortality, and other consequences of suicidal behaviour, based on a public health approach. Also, the World Health Organization issued its first world suicide prevention report in 2014 that called for global suicide prevention from a public health perspective.

A public health approach to suicide prevention focuses on identifying broader patterns of suicide and suicidal behaviour throughout a group or population. This suicide prevention approach is also reflected in an organized five-step process that has been developed for ensuring the effectiveness of preventive efforts. These organized five steps are defining the problem by collecting information about the rates of suicidal behaviours, through a comprehensive surveillance and monitoring system; identifying risk and protective factors for suicide through vigorous research; developing and testing interventions that are safe, ethical, and feasible and aim to maximise success of the program prior to implementation; implementing designed and tested interventions; and evaluating effectiveness of the implemented programs. Evaluation can help determine the particular suicide prevention strategy best fitted to a given circumstance, or how it should be modified in order to achieve maximum effectiveness.

Moreover, to provide a framework for the public health approach in suicide prevention, Mrazek and Hagerty (1994) proposed a prevailing prevention model of universal, selective, and indicated (USI) interventions. This USI model focuses attention on defined populations, from everyone in the population to specific at-risk groups, to specific high-risk individuals—that is, three population groups for whom the designed interventions are deemed optimal for achieving the unique goals of each intervention type. Within this model, universal programs are those that address the general population regardless of risk status, selective programs that address high-risk subgroups within the population, and indicated programs that address high-risk individuals within the population. Although suicide prevention programmes have been implemented in Hong Kong for almost two decades, a structured and well-coordinated suicide prevention strategy is yet to be developed.

It is beyond the scope of this chapter to review all suicide prevention activities around the world. However, it is noteworthy that suicide prevention is likely to be more successful when professional help and social support from people around are available to suicidal individuals. Shneidman clearly points out, 'Suicide prevention is everybody's business.' Although professionals play crucial roles in risk assessment, emergency services, short- and long-term treatments, and research, it should be noted that families and friends are the first line of defence for suicidal individuals in responding to their problems. Therefore, everyone can help preventing suicide by extending care and empathy to those around us. Most suicidal people can be helped in getting through their moments of crisis if they have someone who will take them seriously, listen, provide undivided attention in a non-critical manner without trying to advise or intrude, help them talk about their thoughts and feelings, and offering empathetic and unconditional friendship.

The unique role of the police negotiation cadre in suicide prevention in Hong Kong

Hong Kong is a Special Administrative Region in China covering 1,106.42 square kilometres, with a population of more than 7.45 million. Only 25 per cent of the land in Hong Kong is developed. More than 40 per cent of the land is reserved for country parks and nature reserves, and consequently almost 100 per cent of the population in Hong Kong live in developed areas of 6,830 people per square kilometre, with multiple high-rise buildings. Unofficial figures find that Hong Kong ranks first in the world in numbers of skyscrapers and tall, multistorey buildings, with more than 7,832 existing buildings.

Jumping from a height is the most common method of suicide in Hong Kong and Singapore, where more than 90 per cent of residents live in high-rise buildings. It is also a common method in other populated Asian cities such as Taipei. The method is particularly common amongst older citizens, because it is easily accessible, assuredly lethal, and technically simple for physically fragile older adults residing in tall buildings. Jumping from residential buildings is also commonly adopted by youths whose suicides are impulsive.

In one of my suicide studies using a coroner's court files, I examined suicides by jumping in Hong Kong that occurred between 1 January 2002 and 31 December 2007. It was found that within the study period, the coroner recorded 6,125 suicides with known ages and places of death. Jumping accounted for 2,964 deaths (48.4 per cent); other methods included hanging, strangulation, and suffocation (N = 1,323; 21.6 per cent) and exposure to gases (mainly carbon monoxide) and vapours (N = 1,323, 21.6 per cent). The vast majority (2,521, 85 per cent) of suicides by jumping in Hong Kong occurred at residential sites: 1,501 (50.6 percent) occurred from within decedents' apartments, 292 (9.9 per cent) from the same floor, and 552 (18.6 per cent) from the same building or housing estate. Only a small percentage involved jumping from heights in public areas (5.3 per cent), hospitals (1.1 per cent), and holiday houses (1.6 per cent). The very high proportion of suicides by jumping occurred from decedents' apartment or nearby residential settings is consistent with findings from Bern, New York, and Taipei, where high-rise buildings are prevalent.

It is now well established that means restriction is a highly effective method of suicide prevention. A recent meta-analytic study found that structural interventions at suicide 'hotspots' can avert jumping suicides at these sites. It is documented around the world that erecting physical barriers in public areas, such as bridges and railways, can reduce the number of highly public ('iconic') deaths occurring at those sites. However, with respect to reducing the overall suicide rate in Hong Kong, residential jumping in Hong Kong should be considered as an entirely different phenomenon than jumping suicides at public places and hotspots, because jumping suicide here is far too common, is ecologically embedded, and mainly occurs at the deceased's own apartments. This phenomenon highlights the potential challenges in implementing restriction of means in reducing regional suicide rates.

It is unfortunate that the ubiquity of high-rise buildings in Hong Kong may limit the opportunity to employ means restriction for jumping suicides at residential high-rise buildings as a major suicide-prevention strategy. However, because of its high visibility, when a person chooses to die by suicide from jumping in Hong Kong, he or she would normally climb out of a window from his/her own residency or go to the roof of the building. Also, where physical distances between buildings and between people are small, when compared with suicide attempts by gun and hanging, suicides by jumping from a height in Hong Kong are more easily noticed by others and reported for rescuing. Hence, police officers play a very significant role in preventing suicide in Hong Kong because they are usually the first party to be called to try to effect rescues. Of those who are seriously contemplating suicide and struggling between the wishes of dying and living at the jumping spots, the Police Negotiation Cadre (PNC) of the Hong Kong Police (HKP) will be called upon to negotiate with the 'voice of death' within that person. The PNC is invariably the last resort in preserving that person's life.

Conclusion

Suicide has been called a permanent solution to a temporary problem. Moreover, this permanent solution affects many people afterwards. It is painful to know that every day in Hong Kong, there are people who choose this so-called solution to escape their problems. I certainly have no ready antidotes to the high incidence of suicide in Hong Kong. However, I am committed to contributing to any initiative which seeks to preserve human life. I am honoured, humbled, and very grateful to be invited to write a chapter in this book. I hope that the efforts of the PNC in suicide prevention in Hong Kong will inspire many of our readers and help them understand that they as individuals, through being aware of the symptoms and behaviours of people at risk of suicide, and through being prepared to listen empathetically and give unconditional support, can become frontline warriors in the fight against suicide. People who commit or who are contemplating suicide are not strangers, are not statistics. They can be our children, parents, families, friends, and work colleagues.

Dr Paul Wai-Ching Wong D.Psyc (Clinical), RegClinPsyc (Australia), RCP (HKPS), FHKPsS, MAPS
Associate Professor and Clinical Psychologist
Honorary Research Fellow, Hong Kong Police College
Department of Social Work and Social Administration
Faculty of Social Sciences, the University of Hong Kong.
Email: paulw@hku.hk.

Part A:

BACKGROUND INFORMATION AND DEFINITIONS

Chapter One

The Police Negotiation Cadre, Hong Kong Police Force

Background

The Police Negotiation Cadre (PNC) of the Hong Kong Police is a unit comprising of police officers trained in crisis negotiation. The cadre provides round-the-clock call-out service to resolve crises through negotiation. It is a volunteer secondary duty. Chief superintendent Gilbert Wong was commanding officer of the cadre between January 2010 and December 2021. Upon his retirement from the HK Police Force in December 2021, senior superintendent Stephen Liauw succeeded Gilbert as the commanding officer. He is assisted by three deputies. They are chief superintendent Chi Kwong Wong, chief superintendent Paul Ng and senior superintendent Steve Li. The cadre came into being in 1975, originally as a segment of the police force's counterterrorism response mechanism. As time evolved, the cadre has expanded its capabilities to handle would-be suicides, barricaded sieges, and public order–related incidents.

The Police Negotiation Cadre logo

What does the logo signify? Gilbert explains that starting at the bottom, the hands of Mother Nature come together and use her/his palms to cup intertwined leaves of the wreath. The leaves of the wreath symbolise members of the cadre. They nurture and support each other. They hold a firm belief that 'Who Cares Wins'.

What is the essence of this care and a win? Every crisis negotiator cares that no life is inconsequential. Thus, he/she negotiates to bring resolution, hope, safety, and peace in a crisis where any life is at stake, because every life matters. The two Chinese words 談判, meaning negotiation, stand right at the middle-high ground and the grand entrance/exit of the wreath. Through negotiation, it is hoped to bring peace to those who feel tangled up in the turmoil of reality. A dove, a symbol of peace, nests in this goblet of 'Who Cares Wins'. In its beak, the dove carries a keychain of the PNC. The three characters stand for passion, nobility, and commitment, the intrinsic values that each crisis negotiator beholds. These values nurture and strengthen them. That is the win.

We invite the reader to read the crisis negotiators' declaration, which is included as part of the front matter in this book.

A logo of the Police Negotiation Cadre.

Recruitment and training

The cadre conducts recruitment exercises every two years. Initially, only individuals of the rank of inspector or above could apply to join the cadre. Since 2001, enlistment has been extended to junior officers from the rank and file. Interested police officers have to complete a detailed application form. The first phase is a shortlisting, in order to select about a hundred potential candidates from amongst several hundred applications. Shortlisted applicants have to undergo a one-day selection exercise. They have to give an impromptu talk, handle simulated crisis incidents such as attempted suicide and barricade incidents, and participate in listening exercises relating to a simulated crisis. The applicants will then complete a tailor-made written psychological assessment. A team of police clinical psychologists review the results. From there, the number of suitable candidates will be further refined. The remaining candidates will attend a final interview. Successful candidates will undergo a comprehensive and intensive two-week training course of 160 hours. The training hours involve intensive lectures in the daytime and then simulated exercises in the evening. These exercises typically last until midnight. The long hours of training are intended to test trainees' tolerance levels and mental perseverance. Trainees have to cope with long working hours and fatigue. Occasionally, some trainees cannot cope with the pressure or are considered not suitable for various reasons. The trainers then patiently explain to them the reasons that they are deemed unsuitable to continue the training.

Upon completion of the course, the newly graduated PNC members will be on stand-by duty for two weeks every month, for the first six months. Whenever they attend a scene, an experienced PNC member will work with them and provide guidance. In this way, every new PNC member will have ample opportunities to handle real-life crisis scenarios under the guidance of a mentor.

From time to time, the PNC conducts in-house training. Specialists from overseas crisis negotiation teams, such as the Federal Bureau of Investigations (FBI) of the United States, the metropolitan police of the United Kingdom, the Scotland police force, the Australian federal police force, and the Singapore police force are invited to Hong Kong to run thematic courses.

The Hong Kong police also nominate cadre members to attend overseas crisis negotiation courses organised by these counterparts. In October 2017, a class of seventeen police officers of different ranks completed a two-week crisis negotiation course (CNC) (The Newspaper of the Hong Kong Police Force, Off Beat Issue no. 1100, *Officers Join PNC After Taking Crisis Negotiation Course*). Apart from local police officers, five members of local and overseas law enforcement agencies—Hong Kong fire services department, Hong Kong immigration department, Macao judiciary police, Singapore police force, and Singapore prison services—also participated in the course. Such is the stature of the course that the Hong Kong University's school of professional and continuing education has been recognised as satisfying the requirements for the awarding of a postgraduate diploma in public order (crisis negotiation). The diploma has been given level six qualification, which is equivalent to master level under the Hong Kong qualifications framework'.

Structure of the PNC

The head of the cadre is a commanding officer. He is assisted by three deputy officers who oversee the overall management of the PNC. Besides them, a chief research and development officer (CR&D) and a chief training officer (CTO) are responsible for conducting academic research and designing training programmes. Cadre members are assigned to four teams. They are on the roster to respond to call-outs round the clock. As of December 2021, the cadre has 101 members.

Operational mechanism in a crisis scenario

When handling a crisis, three groups of personnel form a triangular framework. They work and liaise closely together with the common goal of saving lives and peacefully resolving crisis. They are the police incident commander, the tactical team, and the police negotiation cadre.

The uniformed police officers of the division where the incident occurs will respond to the incident. A police incident commander, usually at inspectorate rank, will be in charge overall.

Any police officer can request the PNC to attend a scene and assist in defusing a crisis. Such a request is made through the police regional command and control centre, which then contacts the on-call PNC team. The crisis negotiator communicates with the subject person, apprises the incident commander of the progress, and recommends the appropriate course of action. Every person takes up different roles.

In the Hong Kong police force, the emergency unit provides an immediate response to emergency reports that are reported via the 999 phone line. Five emergency units serve the five police land regions, namely Hong Kong Island, Kowloon East, Kowloon West, New Territories North, and New Territories South. On top of the standard police equipment, these officers are equipped with additional protective gear and door-breaking equipment. At the scene of a crisis incident, they come under the command of the police incident commander.

Equipment of a PNC team

Maintaining effective communication is key to negotiation. A dialogue is only meaningful if both parties can hear it. To overcome physical constraints such as distance and noisy surroundings, in 2006, the PNC team has designed and developed a negotiation throw-ball ('the ball'). It is so named because of the round metal cage that protects the electronic equipment inside.

The ball has several functions. It is round in shape so that it can be rolled over a distance on the ground to reach a subject person. A cable is attached to the ball. The negotiator's voice is capable of being transmitted and amplified by the device. On the other hand, the subject's talk can be captured by the device and transferred back to the negotiator. The device has a built-in camera to transmit visual images of the surrounding area to the PNC team at the site. Because it is not for evidence gathering, the camera has no recording function.

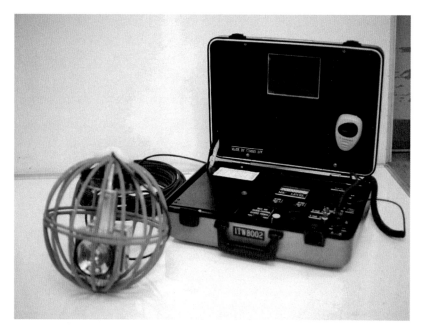

A picture of a set of negotiation throw-ball equipment.

A picture of a negotiation throw-ball.

In past incidents, some individuals did not like having such a device near them. One man tried to cut the cable. Another covered the ball with a jacket to block communication. The functioning of the ball has undergone major improvements over the years. The sound quality and screen resolution have been enhanced; the technical team has developed a stick that can be attached to the ball and extended to a maximum length of 2.7 metres. The stick is sturdier than the cable. The metal casing has been replaced with a plastic one for better, overall safety. The total weight of the whole device has been further reduced.

International Police Negotiators Working Group conference (INWG)

The International Police Negotiators Working Group conference (INWG) was first convened by the FBI in 2000. It is an international network of crisis negotiators from over thirty police forces in the world. It is a well-established and recognised international forum which discusses key issues and promotes good practices in crisis and hostage negotiation. It is held every year in one of the participating regions or countries.

The Hong Kong Police Negotiation Cadre hosted one of the annual conferences in Hong Kong in 2007. (The Newspaper of the Hong Kong Police Force, Off Beat no. 960, *PNC Delegation Attends INWG Annual Conference*).

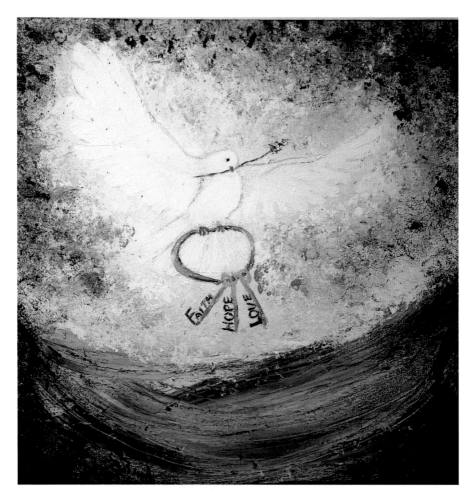

A painting, 'Dove', by Karma Castilho.

A dove delivers a flower of peace that brings faith, hope, and love to the troubled souls. This has a strong affinity with the mission of the Police Negotiation Cadre to preserve life and lead sufferers to come to realise that after the darkness, there is the light of a better future.

Chapter Two

The Art and Morality
of Negotiation

In Gilbert's twenty-two years of experience in the police negotiation cadre (PNC), he has tackled close to one thousand
crisis situations. In his role, he has read extensively in related
academic literature. He has attended many professional training
courses and conferences, including the flagship national academy programme offered by the Federal Bureau of Investigation
(FBI) in the United States. By combining his academic knowledge
with his empirical practices, he offers several ways in which to
interpret negotiation. For easier understanding, acronyms and
initialism are used to present the concepts.

You may ask, 'What is negotiation?' The elements of negotiation
might well be considered through the use of two acronyms, ASK
and NEGOTIATION.

ASK

A stands for attitude. A crisis negotiator will have a caring personality and is genuinely interested in helping people. He/she
holds a positive outlook on life and is able to remain calm and
composed when working under intense pressure.

S stands for skill. A crisis negotiator will be capable of understanding and digesting the training provided and be able to master a wide spectrum of skills in real-life scenarios in—for example, communication, influence and persuasion, and negotiation.

K stands for knowledge. A crisis negotiator will work with his/her team to gather information about the person in crisis. The information may be obtained from, for example, family, friends, neighbours, and observers. The information gathered can assist the negotiator in understanding the subject person and engaging in active listening, with respect to issues pertinent to the situation. An intelligence-led negotiation greatly enhances the effectiveness of a negotiation.

There is an abundance of academic texts on this ASK model. It refers to the attitude, skill, and knowledge that a person needs in order to be competent in a profession, a field of studies, and the like.

NEGOTIATION

By breaking up the word *negotiation* into several compartments—ne/go/ti/ation—it is not difficult to grasp the whole process of negotiation.

Ne stands for Need. The negotiator has to consider his/her own need and the need of the subject person. Every human has needs. Abraham Maslow, one of the most influential psychologists in the twentieth century, has categorised these into five hierarchies: self-actualisation, esteem, love/belonging, safety, and physiological. They are arranged in a pyramid diagram with physiological need at the bottom. There is an abundance of academic literature on Maslow's theory.

The issue of needs applies both to the person threatening suicide and to the negotiator, who is trying to preserve that person's life. If a person's needs are understood by a negotiator, then that negotiator is in a much better position to affect a positive outcome in negotiation. The negotiator needs to be able to assess her/his own needs, especially as they relate to material needs, technical support, intelligence, and backup support from colleagues.

With respect to need, how to react to a subject or negotiator's need for a call of nature, and whether to allow the subject to rest due to fatigue, can be an opportunity or a cause for concern. On the part of the subject, it may present a window of opportunity to effect a behavioural change—that is, to surrender or abort the suicidal attempt. On the other hand, it may instead heighten an imminent danger—for instance, if a person is standing on a ledge of the outer wall of a high-rise building. The person may lose balance and fall accidentally, due to anxiety or distress caused by that physical need or because she/he has a diminished sense of danger and ability to physically negotiate that danger. Whether to allow a person to rest or relieve himself/herself can be a strategic issue. The negotiator must make a determination as to whether the supplication to rest or relieve oneself is likely to prolong the crisis situation or provide an opportunity to bring the event to a positive close. If a negotiator needs to take a break, he/she will inform the subject person and provide a replacement.

Go stands for Goal. The subject person's goal may be to end his/her life, to kill a captive along with killing himself/herself, or to use the death threat as a means of coercing a third party to carry out an action that that person doesn't want to do. The negotiator strives to build rapport and get to know the subject person and his/her goals and intentions. The negotiator seeks to achieve this goal of his/her own through the dynamics of active listening. Ultimately, the negotiator hopes to effect a change in the subject person's mood and general mindset so the person makes a choice to abort the suicide attempt or dangerous act.

Ti stands for Time. Time is an important factor in any negotiation. Sometimes negotiation is like running a marathon. There are actual cases in the past where a negotiation continues for long hours and even overnight. Any progress that occurs does so incrementally, in stages, which may only be discerned by an experienced negotiator. With respect to time, the exact opposite situation might manifest itself. Consider, for example, the scenario of an elderly person who is sitting on the top of an air-conditioner, on the outer wall of a high-rise building. Two out of the four screws of the supporting frame have already come loose. Rescue action needs to kick in immediately. The negotiator may not have much time to build rapport and can only try his/her best to calm the suicidal person and give him/her instructions with respect to securing his/her safety.

Ation stands for Action. Action consists of strategic and tactical action. The PNC team, the police incident commander, and the tactical team work closely together to formulate a strategy and action plan. The PNC team regularly updates the incident commander with respect to the progress of the negotiation, taking into consideration both the time and need factors.

When a subject person agrees to abort his/her dangerous intent, the negotiator needs to consider the best course of action which will ensure that the person is taken out of the physical danger that she/he has put herself/himself in. Is the person able to walk or climb back to a place of safety without assistance? Are firemen needed to rescue the subject person? If the negotiation is not progressing well and the subject person displays signs that he/she may be readying himself/herself to carry out his/her threats, does the tactical team or firemen proceed with immediate rescue action, even without consent of the subject person?

These four elements are very fluid and interchangeable in a negotiation situation. Their effective application hinges very much on the PNC and incident commander's combined judgement and the unique circumstances of the case.

Eight Cs model

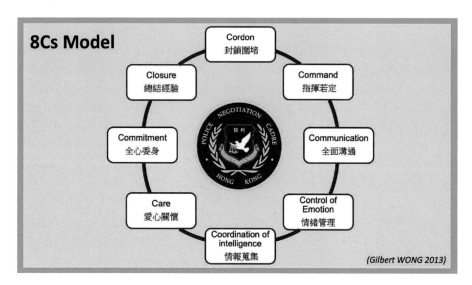

A diagram of an Eight-Cs model

From a wider perspective, negotiation is teamwork, which involves all the stakeholders in a crisis situation. Gilbert had initially developed a five Cs model, and it eventually became six and seven. According to him, the purpose of developing this model is to provide a user-friendly mind map for frontline police officers as a quick reference because they are often the first persons to respond to a crisis incident. It also provides a strategic framework for an incident commander to monitor the negotiation process. Subsequently, Gilbert has expanded the model to the eight Cs.

The eight Cs are cordon, command, communication, control of emotion, coordination of intelligence, care, commitment, and closure.

Cordon consists of both physical cordon and verbal cordon (also referred to as containment). The uniformed police officers who first arrive at the scene will cordon off the area and prohibit unrelated personnel from entering. An effective cordon will isolate the scene from unnecessary interference from members of the public or the media. It is like the process of sterilisation which occurs in an operational theatre before surgery is to be performed.

The negotiator talks positively, in order to achieve verbal containment. He/she guides or steers the subject person to listen to what the negotiator has to say. Conversely, the subject person is guided to talk to the negotiator. If, during a negotiation, the subject person starts to trail off or makes an attempt to jump off a building, the negotiator may shout 'Come back!' or 'Don't move!' in an affirmative tone. Such a simple command can affect a psychological response on the part of the person, compelling him/her to become attentive or desist from resorting to an attempt at suicide.

Command refers to the overall command and decision-making when handling a crisis situation. Crisis negotiation management involves three entities: the police incident commander, the tactical team, and the police negotiation team. The incident commander is responsible for the whole operation. He/she communicates closely with the other two entities and makes decision on the basis of what she/he knows about the changing circumstances in a negotiation. An overall commander will not engage in negotiation. Conversely, a negotiator does not take up a commanding or decision-making role.

A commander oversees the operation and distributes and co-ordinates resources. He/she will make the decision whether to scale down an operation or call for more manpower, as the situation warrants. Each entity has its own team leader, who coordinates its own resources, logistics, or replacements.

Communication refers to the negotiator's communication with the subject person, as well as with other units responsible for resolving the crisis. The PNC team will provide useful information to the negotiator to facilitate meaningful communication with the subject person. The negotiator employs active listening skills to find out what has happened to trigger the crisis, what matters most, and what issues to avoid mentioning. The communication process accommodates and accepts the subject person as he/she is, without being judgemental. When that person in crisis feels that he/she is being understood and accepted, he/she starts to open up and gradually becomes receptive to coping strategies offered by the negotiator. The effectiveness of soft communication (active listening) should never be underestimated.

Control of emotion follows hand in hand with communication. Through non-judgemental and empathetic communication, the negotiator acknowledges the subject person's difficulties, anger, or sense of hopelessness. If the subject mentions some positive incidents or moments, the negotiator may focus on those issues and encourage the person to elaborate upon them. In the process, the person's negative and destructive emotion may be moderated, and at the same time the rational thinking mode kicks in. In that transitional period, the person may gradually become more receptive to coping strategies offered by the negotiator. In Gilbert's words, control of emotion through communication is 100 per cent science as well as 100 per cent art.

Coordination of intelligence encompasses collation, assessment, and analysis of all information collected from all possible sources. Such information may come from the person, his/her friends, neighbours, or even bystanders. Effective coordination of intelligence has the potential to provide a good picture of the whole incident—for example, why such a person appears on such a date and time, at such a location, behaving in such a way. Hopefully it also provides some insights into how to resolve the crisis. The PNC team analyses and filters the information and then feeds useful and timely intelligence to the negotiator to facilitate the negotiation. It is an intelligence-led communication and negotiation.

Care is an intrinsic element in crisis negotiation. In the Hong Kong scenarios, the negotiator usually talks to the subject person face to face. The negotiator communicates in an empathetic tone with positive body language. Very often, care and being listened to is what the subject lacks and yearns for.

Commitment refers to the perseverance of a negotiator in her/his mission to prioritise the saving of life through the process of negotiation. It goes no matter whether the subject person is a drug addict or a notorious criminal, or whether the person is hostile towards the police or negotiator. A negotiator upholds an unwavering belief that no life is inconsequential. This is one of the core values of the PNC, which are passion, nobility, and commitment.

Closure consists of three parts: operational debriefing, psychological debriefing, and experience sharing. At the conclusion of a crisis situation, the PNC team will hold an operational debriefing as soon as practicable to review the whole process. The teammates acknowledge each other's good work and explore areas in which they can improve the efficacy of their work. This occurs while the details are still fresh in their minds. It is essential for the team leader to check with each and every member to ensure that psyches have not been weakened or damaged by specific events which occurred during the course of negotiations. Such issues can be very personal and may be experienced by only one member of the team. Again, if a person ends his/her life in the end, sometimes right in front of the negotiator, it is crucial for the team to offer each other care and support. If necessary, the team may seek help and counselling from the police clinical psychologist. Lastly, the team collates the learning points for incorporation into future training sessions, to provide relevant data for future research as well as refine the standard operation procedures, if appropriate.

This eight Cs model can be interpreted under ASK: A for attitude that covers care and commitment; S for skill that covers cordon, control of emotion, and coordination of intelligence; and K for knowledge that covers command, communication, and closure. Gilbert reiterates that the division and order are not absolute. Individual circumstances dictate what will be employed first.

In a nutshell, all the narratives have all the elements of the eight Cs model. They are categorised under a specific C to exemplify the special qualities of that C. More often than not, a story could be appropriately placed under a number of C headings.

PNC

PNC is the abbreviation for the Police Negotiation Cadre. Using PNC as an initialism, it can stand for passion, nobility, and commitment. Those are the core values that every police negotiator holds.

A painting, 'Rejuvenation', by Karma Castilho.

The sunlight's energy and warmth nurtures the earth. A seed of the parent tree has burst through. A new life is ignited. The roots are anchored deep into the earth. The seedling will grow and mature into a strong tree. The painting is a metaphorical representation of the deep belief of the members of the police negotiation cadre that after darkness and seeming hopelessness, hope, optimism, and joy can emerge and prosper in the human psyche once more.

Part B:

THE FIRST C—CORDON

Chapter Three

It Is Not What You Say but How You Say It (Barricade)

Crisis negotiator Gilbert Wong

When you see a person acting and shouting irrationally, what can you do to calm him/her down?

On an evening in mid-2018, such a scenario occurred. Uniformed branch police officers had cordoned off part of a pedestrian walkway and a section of the road outside a convenience store in Kowloon. Inside the store, an English-speaking Asian male was shouting and wielding a four-inch-long cutter. A tactical team, the emergency unit (EU) of Kowloon West Region, was at the scene to handle the situation. They were fully armed with shields and batons.

Behind the police cordons were the media reporters and curious bystanders trying to ascertain what was going on.

'Calm down! Calm down! Put down the knife immediately!' shouted one policeman.

'What? Why do I have to listen to you? All of you, go away!' the man replied in a defiant tone. He then took off his shirt. Distinct abrasion lines appeared on his chest as he ran the sharp blade of the cutter over his body. Gasps of 'Oh!' and muffled screams could be heard from the crowd.

'Hey, hey! Man, stop! Relax! Calm down! Put the knife down!'

'Stop! Calm down!'

'Put the knife down!'

'Calm down! Put the knife down!'

A chorus of EU officers' commanding voices was directed at the man, who became more agitated. The atmosphere was highly charged.

Gilbert Wong, in his capacity as a police negotiator, was notified to attend the scene. He was a chief superintendent of police (CSP) at the time of this incident.

The negotiator received more information on the way to the scene. The man had assaulted and injured another man during an earlier argument. He tried to elude the pursuing police officers. The negotiator walked to the front of the police cordon line and spoke calmly to the tactical team officers. 'OK, all of you. Listen to me. Stop all talking and shouting this minute. Let me handle this. Let me walk in front of you. I will talk to the man.'

'Uh … yes, sir. But let us shield you—it's too dangerous for you to walk to the front. The man is armed!' one police officer of the tactical team responded hesitantly. The negotiator acknowledged the officer's concern and nodded reassuringly as he walked to the front. They accepted the negotiator's authority but remained on high alert, standing close behind him, ready to rush to his aid should it be necessary.

Though appearing calm and relaxed, the negotiator kept a vigilant eye on the cutter in the man's hand. He was mentally prepared to evade any sudden thrust by the man.

The negotiator spoke calmly to the Asian man in English. 'Hello, mister. I am Wong. I am here to help resolve this situation. Calm down. Calm down.' He said these words calmly and slowly. 'While I am here, nobody is going to hurt you. I would like to know what happened and to listen to what you have to say.'

'I don't know nothing! I don't know nothing! Everybody is crazy! They won't listen to me!' the man continued to rant without providing any specific information. For a time, he continued his tirade.

Then the negotiator said, 'You have a lot of things to say. Can I walk closer to you? I need your permission to come closer. I need your guarantee that you will not hurt me. See for yourself: I have no weapon with me. I want to know what has happened. The police officers will stand right behind me. They will not walk past me without my instruction.'

The man's demeanour became calmer. 'OK, come forward.' The man alleged that he had wanted to buy a drink at that convenience store. He asked the cashier a few questions in English. The cashier waved him away and refused his request. The man did not understand why he was being treated in that way. Frustrated, he grabbed a cutter that lay near the cashier's counter and started yelling at people.

'I have money to pay for the drink. Nobody believes me. Do you believe me? Do you believe me?' the man spoke angrily. Without waiting for the negotiator's reply, the man hit his forehead against a glass cabinet in the shop. Immediately there was bleeding from his forehead.

'Hey, man, I never said that I don't believe you. Calm down. How are you? Are you feeling all right? I will not hurt you. Can you put away the cutter?' the negotiator maintained an even and assuring tone.

The man put down the cutter.

'Want some water? Take this one. I'll have one too.' As the negotiator said this, he took two bottles of water from a shelf and offered one to the man.

'Thank you. I will pay. I have money,' the man said.

The negotiator offered to pay instead.

'No, no, no. I pay. I pay.' The man was very determined to pay for the drinks. The negotiator instructed the cashier to accept the payment.

Meanwhile, the negotiator walked the man to a corner farther inside the shop. At that location, the tactical team was able to tighten its cordon and prepare to make the arrest.

The man had some water. They talked a bit more. At length, the negotiator restored a sense of reality to the man. The police officers had to arrest him because he had assaulted a person. The man was silent for a while and then nodded. But he had two conditions before he would assent to his arrest. He would only allow the negotiator to make the arrest, not those police officers in uniform. Also, he wished to have a few puffs of a cigarette. There was no problem with the cigarette, but the arrest by the negotiator was not so easily done.

'Officer, hand over your pair of handcuffs to me. Unlock them first,' the negotiator said. In his mind, he was frantically going over the correct procedures which had to be followed to arrest and handcuff an individual. The last time he needed to do that was at least twenty years ago, when he was a young inspector of police.

'Yes, sir,' the uniformed police officer standing closest to the negotiator responded hesitatingly. He looked confused that a chief superintendent was doing the job that he should be doing instead.

After the negotiator locked one wrist of the man with a handcuff, the man held onto the other handcuff with his free hand. This sudden act startled the police officers nearby, and they closed in. They thought that the man was trying to put up a struggle.

'I need to handcuff your other hand as well,' the negotiator told the man.

'Can you just handcuff one hand, and I hold the other half of the handcuff?'

'Uh, not really. I have to handcuff both hands,' the negotiator told the man calmly, and he completed the handcuffing. He escorted the man out of the shop, with the tactical team officers close behind. The media's cameras were on them as they made their way out to the police car. Once the man was inside the police vehicle, the negotiator spoke to the police incident commander. 'Hey, when the guy is away from the reporters, please arrange for him to have a few puffs of a cigarette.'

'Sir, that would not be a very good idea. Do you really mean it?'

'Look, I promised the guy earlier on. Just do me this favour!'

The incident commander agreed reluctantly and honoured his promise.

Gilbert's reflection

Gilbert arrived at the scene where both the subject person and the attending police officers were shouting at each other. An excited and curious crowd of bystanders added extra pressure for the police officers. The tension was escalating. He first needed to calm down all the parties. He had sufficient experience that enabled him to instruct the nervous police officers to cease all talking and open a path for him to walk to the front. He also had the tactical team right behind to protect him.

His friendly approach had a calming effect on the subject person. He was engaged in active listening and facilitated the subject person to vent his anger and tell his side of the story. Eventually, the subject person was able to rationalise the situation and agreed to surrender.

Calming an agitated and armed man is an important aspect in negotiation. A negotiator bears in mind the body posture, pace of the dialogue, choice of words, tone of voice, facial expression, and hand gestures. He/she builds up these skills through practice, observation, and experience sharing. Every situation has its unique challenges and calls upon flexible application of classroom theory and practice.

Cordon

The incident occurred in a busy area with lots of bystanders. The uniformed police officers and the tactical team effectively cordoned off the area. In this localised scenario, the negotiator was able to do what he had to do. At the same time, the tactical team was in the innermost cordon, to protect the negotiator in case of any sudden emergency.

Chapter Four

To Authenticate a Police Negotiator (Attempted Suicide)

Crisis negotiator Ken Fung (Kuen)

If a person asks, 'What proof do you have to convince me you are an authentic police negotiator?' how does a police negotiator convince the man with respect to his identity?

On a day around four in the morning, the visitors' area of the Mong Kok police station was filled with people waiting their turn to make reports. Suddenly a few persons screamed when they saw a man bleeding from his neck. He had cut himself with a broken piece of glass. While sitting at a corner at the visitors' area, he shouted at the approaching uniformed police officers to stay away. The police officer of Mong Kok police station had requested the attendance of the Police Negotiation Cadre (PNC) with a view to defuse the crisis. At the same time, the tactical team, an emergency unit of Kowloon west region (EU KW), was on their way to the scene.

Ken Fung had joined the PNC in 2015. He was a sergeant at the time of handling the incident. He was working in the EU KW, and on that night, he was on duty. The unit serves the police districts in Kowloon west police region. The unit responds to requests from the districts for handling emergency incidents such as attempted suicide.

Since Ken was a trained PNC member, and his supervisor instructed him to handle the incident in his capacity as a police negotiator whilst the PNC on-call team was on their way.

Ken decided to change into civilian clothes before approaching the man. It is one of the small but important details that can facilitate easier rapport building between the negotiator and the person in a crisis situation.

The operational base of EU KW is at the Mong Kok police district. Ken returned his police equipment (beat radio, firearm, baton, OC foam, and handcuffs) to the armoury at that station. Here, it was also convenient for him to change into civilian clothes, because the kit locker of EU KW officers is in the same building with the police station.

A uniformed police officer had previously talked to the man. The man was in his early thirties. He used to run a trading business. At his business partner's urging, he was asked to contribute more and more capital towards the business. He did so, but the company lost money and ceased trading. He tried to find work, but the resultant pay cheques were barely enough to cover the family expenses. Moreover, his employer owed him more than two months' salary. Consequently, the man was in debt. His parents and in-laws blamed him for this fact. He and his wife quarrelled frequently over money matters.

When Ken arrived at the report room, the tactical team officers had already cordoned off the area and cleared it of all bystanders. The duty officer had redirected members of the public to attend an alternative police station.

A uniformed police officer spoke to the man. 'Hey, man, you say you will only talk to a police negotiator. Here he is.'

'You? Ha! Are you kidding me? I know you people. Don't play games with me. You are either a task force or special duty squad guy[1], the man scoffed.

Ken realised he had a problem. Normally he wore smart casual wear whenever he attended a crisis situation in his capacity as a PNC member; a shirt with no tie, long pants, and non-sports shoes was his preferred choice. His PNC team was not on roster call that week, so he was in a T-shirt and denim pants. Officers of a task force subunit or special duty squad usually dress that way to blend in with people on the streets. It is also convenient to lay an ambush or run around in such casual attire.

Ken noted with mild surprise that the man had some knowledge of different units in the police force.

'I will not trust police officers anymore. I only trust police negotiators. Find one for me. I want to talk to him.'

'I am a police negotiator, 100 per cent. It has never occurred to me that I need to prove my identity. Perhaps you can talk to me, and I shall see how I can help you,' Ken responded.

'I don't believe you. The way you dress, you must be a task force guy. You don't even have an assistant to take notes for you.'

'I do have an assistant. Hey, brother, you, over here. Stay close behind me. Don't stand so far away. See? He is my assistant. He has been taking notes for me.' Because the on-call PNC team was still on its way, Ken had requested a uniformed police officer from his EU team to be his temporary assistant and jot down

---

[1]   A police district headquarters comprises of one or more police divisions. A police district has a special duty squad (SDS). There are usually three SDS teams. They are responsible for combating vice, illegal gambling, and dangerous drugs activities in the district. Each police division has a task force subunit responsible for combating local crime problems.

notes for him. *This man must have watched police negotiators at work in the past*, Ken thought.

'You are bluffing. Don't waste my time. Find me a police negotiator.'

While they were talking, Ken felt someone tap him on the shoulder. He looked back with relief as his PNC team partner had arrived.

'Hello, mister. I am a police negotiator, and so is my partner here. Just a moment; I'll show you something.' As the PNC team partner greeted the man, he took out his mobile phone and scrolled through the phone's photo album. 'Look at this photo on my phone. Do you recognise this guy in the photo? It's him, my partner here. This is a recruitment poster inviting police officers to join our cadre. Ken, this man standing before you, was being photographed in his police negotiator's outfit in this poster. Do you see that? We are both authentic police negotiators. No bluffing at all. Trust us. The outfit we wear is for publicity. We do not wear it when we attend the scene to talk to people whom we try to help.'

維護法紀 你我承擔
SERVE AND PROTECT OUR HONG KONG
警察招募熱線:2860 2860
www.police.gov.hk/recruitment

A recruitment poster of the Police Negotiation Cadre, Hong Kong Police. The poster depicted Ken (second from the left) and another PNC member talking to a distraught person. Standing beside them were two uniformed police officers of the Hong Kong Police.

'Ah, I see. OK.' From then on, the man agreed to talk to Ken.

Slowly, the man talked about the days when his business was thriving. His parents-in-law, uncles, and aunts had envied him and showered him with praise. However, when things began to turn downhill, his relatives and friends turned their backs on him. He drank to drown his problems. The more he drank, the more he became embroiled in a vicious cycle of self-pity.

One evening, he was very drunk. He approached a policeman on the street and requested that he refer him to some psychological counselling service. The police officer sent him to a hospital. As far as he could remember, the hospital staff arranged a place for him to rest and then discharged him as soon as he woke up from his drunken state. They did not provide him with any counselling service.

He was furious with the police, the doctors, his wife, and everybody. On that day, he decided to wreak vengeance. He would kill himself at the busy police station. People would bear witness to his protest against the injustice done to him.

While he was talking, the man suddenly sank to the floor. He shut his eyes, seemingly determined to push the piece of broken glass into his neck.

'Wait, wait, mister. Listen to me. I know that you are feeling very angry and upset. If you die now, what is going to happen to your wife?' As Ken said this, the man ceased his attempt at self-harm and opened his eyes, which were welling up with tears. Ken realised that his wife mattered a lot to him. This was an avenue through which he could establish dialogue with the man. The negotiator continued. 'If you die now, who will protect your wife when people bully her?'

'I love my wife very much. I don't say it out loud, but I truly love her and don't want her to worry about me.' The man sighed heavily.

Ken responded in a supportive tone. 'Yes, you love your wife very much and don't want her to worry about you. I am listening to you. I understand that you are still very upset. Can you lower the piece of broken glass instead of pressing it against your neck? The way you are holding it makes me feel very tense. All I wish you to do is to lower it. I won't take away the broken piece of glass by force.' Silence ensued, and then the man lowered his hand.

'I understand how you are feeling. It is not easy to take this step. You are very brave to have faced so many problems on your own.' While Ken was talking, he held out his hand, an important gesture of assurance. 'I am willing to accompany you to the ambulance and then on to the hospital to see the doctor. We can handle this together. I will tell the doctor that you have been very brave in facing your problems. You are under a lot of pressure. I will also request the doctor refer you for counselling services through the social welfare department.'

'Why should I trust you?' the man asked hesitantly.

'I do not wish you to attempt suicide again. I have no motive to lie to you. I will accompany you all the way to the hospital. My colleagues have stepped aside. A path is opened before you. I'll walk with you.'

It was around six thirty in the morning. There was a short silence. The man placed the piece of broken glass on the floor. The negotiator helped the man to board the ambulance. He shielded the man's face from the reporters' cameras. As promised, the negotiator spoke to the medical doctor in the man's presence.

A few weeks later, the police public relations branch (PPRB) redirected an email to Ken. The email was sent by the man. The gist of the email was as follows.

'I am so very grateful to the police negotiator. He listened so patiently. I felt he truly understood my problems. He talked so sincerely and let me see what treasuring one's life really means. I came to realise that my family mattered a lot to me. In the past, I have formed an incorrect impression of police officers. I wish to thank the police negotiator for saving my life.'

Ken's reflection

Ken was much comforted by the thought that the man would not attempt suicide again. Negotiation is not about crafting dramatic dialogue that persuades the person to give up dying. It is about actively listening and letting the person find his own way to embrace life anew.

Police negotiators do not carry any official identification when they attend a scene. Normally, there is no necessity to prove their identities. This occasion was quite the exception. Fortunately, the problem was resolved quickly.

In this incident, Ken made a point to change into civilian clothes. Not being in uniform set him apart from the attending police officers. A person in distress might respond better to a police negotiator in civilian clothes. He realised that this was a positive strategy based on its use on previous occasions.

Cordon

Mong Kok is a densely populated area and a hugely popular district for shopping, dining, and entertainment by locals and tourists. The Mong Kok police station is situated in this district and is easily accessible by public transport. It is one of the busiest police stations in Hong Kong.

An emotional scene involving a weapon such as this one, occurring in an enclosed and crowded environment, might spin into chaotic scenarios. Therefore, an effective cordon at the initial stage of handling the incident was crucial. The tactical team cordoned off the area instantly to contain the incident. The negotiator could then focus on the task at hand without unnecessary distraction or disruption.

The tactical team also remained on guard in the innermost cordon to protect the negotiator should the occasion arise.

Chapter Five

Beyond Reason (Barricade)

Crisis negotiator Chi Kwong Wong

You and another person have only a ten-feet space between each other. Suddenly, that person rushes towards you. That person's arm is raised, and in his/her hand is a long knife. How long does it take for a human mind to come to the realisation that the end of his/her very life may be at hand? At such an intense moment, does the mind has sufficient time to reach that assessment when the heartbeat doesn't even have time to catch up?

In this particular case, the negotiator's life was a split second away from extinction. He was not saved by chance or coincidence. It was the seamless synthesis of cordon, teamwork, and swift response of the tactical team which ensued that safeguarded the negotiator's life.

Chi Kwong Wong (CK) joined the Police Negotiation Cadre (PNC) in 1999. This case occurred more than ten years ago, and he shared the story with the author in December 2018. The lessons he learned from this experience have a significance and relevance as important now as they were then.

It was well after midnight on a summer day, and the police called CK to attend a scene at a public housing estate in Kowloon. On his way, he received information that a young man was brandishing a long knife and threatening to harm his mother. It was thought that he might be under the influence of some kind of analeptic or psychotropic drug.

The mother opened the door to let the police in. CK, the negotiator, entered the flat. On the righthand side of the unit was a kitchen. A young man in his early twenties was standing at the far end of the kitchen and brandishing a machete. The handle was wrapped in a white cloth. This type of weapon is occasionally used by triads in gang fights in Hong Kong.

The negotiator stood outside the kitchen, some ten feet away from the man. The man was bare-chested. He wore only a pair of sports pants. He noticed the negotiator and swore at him. 'What the f--- are you coming here for?' The man's entire dialogue was laced with expletives.

'Hello, man. The way that you are brandishing a machete frightens people. Your mother is very scared. Can you put it down? I am here to offer you help.'

'I don't need anybody's help! I hate everybody in this world! See? I can do whatever I like. No one can stop me!' The man went on talking irrationally.

The negotiator listened patiently and assessed the situation. He had handled numerous crisis situations before. *This guy is swinging the machete aimlessly. His body posture is not as tense as before. He appears to be slowly letting down his guard. He is not in an attack mode as such. He's ten feet away. I should be able to dodge him if he comes at me*, the negotiator thought. He was confident that he could resolve the crisis.

Around forty-five minutes passed.

'What are you holding that knife for? What made you so angry? You can tell me.'

'Why would you care? I have no job. I've run out of money. I need money. That bitch got money, but she refused to give it to me! Go to hell!' The man continued his rant. He would talk for a while, pause, brandish the machete, and begin talking again. Occasionally he would say, 'Do you believe I would chop you?' The threatening remark was uttered offhandedly. The negotiator was not frightened.

A staged photograph of a man swinging a prop machete.

'Your mom provides you with a place to live. She cooks for you. What do you need the money for? Have you got a job?' The negotiator then paused. The man complained that he got a job before but quit after a month. The salary was low, and the employer was a mean guy. The negotiator felt he had built up a good rapport with the man. He fetched a chair and sat down.

A staged photograph of a negotiator talking to an armed man in a sitting position. Two tactical team officers were standing behind the negotiator to protect him.

'I see, your employer was a mean guy. May be, you can find another —' He did not have a chance to finish his sentence. Suddenly, the youth surged forward and raised the machete above his head. *In a split second, he will reach me.* This was the only thought that filled the negotiator's mind. He sat dead still in his chair, as if accepting his fate. He did not move his arms in self-defence.

Did he feel a rush of adrenaline? Not really. Was he in dire fear? No. He was calm. Why? Such was the suddenness of the young man's attack that the negotiator could not react physically or mentally to the drastically changed circumstances.

What happened within the next second? The negotiator heard a loud cracking sound. Then he saw two armadillo shields slam shut in front of him. Through the transparent shields, he saw a long blade plunging towards him. The cracking sound was the silver blade of the machete hitting forcefully against the shields. The police officers of the emergency unit (EU) thrusted past him and then subdued the youth. CK remained sitting in his chair, still transfixed and in shock. Everything had happened so quickly. Eventually, the man was subdued and taken into custody.

A staged photograph of a man attacking the negotiator with a prop machete. At that instant, two tactical team officers thrusted their armadillo shields in front of the negotiator just in time to block the machete from hitting the negotiator. The negotiator remained frozen in his chair.

The negotiator was to learn later that he was so focused on his negotiation that he had not noticed that the tactical team officers had stationed so closely behind him. The EU officers had all along been on high alert, ready to intervene swiftly should the negotiator's safety become compromised.

CK Wong's reflection

During many experience sharing and training sessions in crisis negotiation, CK shared without hesitation this experience with fellow PNC members and trainees.

When the young man talked more and more about himself, CK felt that they had established a good rapport. He also became used to the sight of the man swinging the machete aimlessly. In his mid-thirties, CK was young and fit. He thought that ten feet would be a sufficient distance for him to respond to an attack, if the man really decided to do so. From the man's speech pattern, CK suspected that he had taken some kind of drug. Otherwise, he was basically talking rationally. He sat down because he wished to convey a message to the man that he was a friendly guy and meant no harm. His assessment of the situation was at odds with the youth's potential for unpredictable and violent behaviour. In hindsight, he had underestimated the risk of the man's erratic behaviour. In a sitting position, he naturally became more vulnerable. His position and the chair itself inhibited his ability to protect himself. Lesson number one: never overrate yourself, no matter how experienced you are.

In movies, a person faced with the prospect of sudden, unexpected death has flashbacks of families and other loved ones. The negotiator had no such experience. The fact was that his body clock remained frozen. One second was simply not a sufficient time for the body or mind to react to a life-threatening assault of such speed and ferocity. Lesson number two: always treat any display of aggression with a lethal weapon with great caution.

To this day, CK still feels immense gratitude to his colleagues for their display of extraordinary bravery and professionalism. He was so focused on the negotiation that he had forgotten about the tactical team's presence. He did not realise that the tactical team officers had cordoned off the corridor and positioned themselves behind him, in a state of high alert.

Cordon

The uniformed police officers had cordoned the area so the negotiator could have an uninterrupted interaction with the youth. In the innermost cordon, the tactical team was in full tactical suit and armed with armadillo shields. The members of the team positioned themselves right behind the negotiator and stayed on high alert to thwart any sudden, unanticipated attack on the part of the youth. Should the subject person decide to surrender, they were there to take him into custody. This scenario was an excellent example of the use of an effective cordon.

Chapter Six

The Point of a Gun (Attempted Suicide)

Case Officer Connie Lee Hamelin

One day in 2006, I was thrown into a situation whereby a police constable appeared in my office with a loaded revolver to his head. It was an alarming situation, but thanks to the training provided by the Hong Kong police force, I did not panic or freeze. I knew what to do.

When a uniformed branch police officer reports for duty, the officer is issued with a service revolver, a Smith and Wesson Model 10, and twelve rounds of ammunition. The revolver can hold a maximum of six rounds of ammunition inside the six cartridge chambers. A police officer is required to fully load her/his revolver and place the remaining six rounds in a speed loader, which is secured to a leather belt of the officer's service uniform. At the end of duty, he/she is required to return all the police equipment, including the revolver, to the armoury.

A picture of a Smith and Wesson revolver Model 10,
and twelve rounds of ammunition. The ammunition
is stored inside two speed loaders.

I was working in the capacity of assistant divisional commander, administration, of a police division in Kowloon. I was a chief inspector. After the daily conference one morning, I was back in my office at around eight, and as was my practice, I had the door open for the convenience of a regular stream of people who would come to discuss matters and deposit or collect documents.

I was reading messages on the computer screen when I heard an indistinct sound coming from the doorway. I did not immediately register that someone was actually talking to me.

'Madam, I wish to die.' These words reached my ears, they were uttered slowly, in a soft, hesitant tone. With fingers poised in mid-air above the computer keyboard, I turned my head towards the source of the sound. For an instant, I was in disbelief.

A senior police constable in uniform was kneeling on the floor at my door. He was holding a revolver in his right hand and pressing the muzzle of the gun against his right temple. It might sound improbable, but my first reaction was to get out of my chair and look around me. I wanted to make sure that the sight before me was real, that this was really happening to me.

The revolver holster was empty. I did not doubt for a second that the police constable had drawn his own service revolver, and I had to assume that it was fully loaded.

Instinctively, my eyes darted towards the constable's right index finger. It rested outside the trigger guard. The muzzle itself was not hard-pressed against his temple. I took these to be good signs that he was perhaps not intent on immediately pulling the trigger.

Careful not to alarm him, I said gently, 'Colleague, you have come to see me.' The police constable repeated his same words, expressing his wish to die.

I scanned the man before me. He was of average build and height, and probably in his fifties. He was still kneeling, his back was slightly hunched, and his eyes were downcast. After walking closer, I lowered myself to his eye level and said in a caring voice, 'Colleague, you appear to be very unhappy. You have come to me for help. I am listening.'

'Madam, no one would help me. I hear that you are a good person.'

'You look worried and distressed. We can tackle your problem together. I would like you to—'

At this juncture, a female senior inspector and a male police constable were walking along the corridor towards my office.

Upon seeing what was going on, they stopped abruptly a few steps away.

I spoke to the police constable in the corridor in a calm and un-hurried tone, 'Inform all personnel on this floor to stay in their offices. Inform the duty officer of the report room to cordon off both ends of this corridor.' I then made a gesture of making a telephone call and pointed upwards. The constable under-stood my cue. He was to inform the senior officers of what was transpiring.

Maintaining the same tone, I continued. 'I am most willing to help you. The way you are holding your revolver makes me feel nervous. I would like you to lower your gun slowly and hand it over to me? Can you do that?' The constable lowered his arm. 'That's right. There's no hurry. Thank you. You have done the right thing. I'm going to take your revolver.' He did not resist.

Once the revolver was in my right hand, I performed the proce-dures smoothly from muscle memory. I pointed the muzzle away from us both and immediately flicked the release latch to open the cylinder. The gun was fully loaded. I pressed once on the ejector with my left thumb, which released the bullets from the chamber, and received the six bullets into my upturned right palm. I slipped the bullets into my uniform dress pocket, got up, and returned to my desk. I put the revolver, with the cylinder still open, inside my desk drawer, locked it, and put the key in my pocket.

In the meantime, the senior inspector helped the police consta-ble stand and had him sit on a two-seater sofa. She sat next to him. I moved an office chair and sat opposite the two of them.

'Have a glass of water. Take a few deep breaths. There is no hurry. Tell me what has led you to take such a step,' I said, keeping my eyes on the constable whilst I put a piece of paper into the hands of the female inspector and indicated she should make a telephone call.

She looked at the paper—*Threat removed, things under control, no injury*—and left my office to report to senior officers at the district headquarters level.

I listened patiently to what the constable had to say. He had joined the police force at the age of twenty. In one or two years, he would reach the official retirement age of fifty-five. At this time, he was working in the transportation fleet of the division. A four-year interdistrict rotation transfer was coming up, and he was on that list.

Every four years, all police officers of the rank and file and inspectorate rank were subject to interdistrict transfer within the same police region.

There is a general practice that if at the time of the transfer exercise, an officer has less than a stipulated amount of time before retirement, he/she can be exempted from the transfer and continue working in the same police district until his/her retirement. The stipulated time is usually one to two years. There may be variation between regions, but this practice is flexible. Besides, police officers also leave the district to serve in other posts for career development or other reasons from time to time.

The constable asked his supervisor to clarify his transfer position and whether he could be exempted from the transfer. He was either told to wait for the reply or to put down his request in writing.

The date of the transfer was drawing close. To work in a new police district would mean an entirely new environment, where he had to get to know a whole new team of colleagues, learn all the street names, and learn and remember all the new driving routes. This stressed him a great deal and led to him suffering from insomnia. That morning, he felt his future was bleak and that nobody cared enough to give him a helping hand. He was determined to end his life with his service revolver. However, he made a last effort to seek help.

I acknowledged his feelings of helplessness. He was almost in tears when I held his hands and assured him that I would speak with his superiors and ascertain the status of the matter. I summoned a colleague to accompany him out of my office and look after him for the time being.

Once he left, a series of follow-up actions were initiated. Foremost, the police constable's supervisor was informed and briefed on how to handle his colleague, given his state of vulnerability. Senior officers at the headquarters level were made aware of the situation.

Subsequently, a special meeting was convened to consider the police constable's welfare. At the same time, a disciplinary enquiry was also set in motion to look into the drawing of a firearm. This act was a serious breach of discipline. A police officer must not draw his/her firearm, with the sole exceptions of preserving his/her own life or that of another person when no other lesser degree of force could achieve these purposes.

Several days later, I interviewed the senior police constable again. This was to assure him of the empathy which I felt for his situation, and to let him know about the disciplinary enquiry. It was essential to conduct a reality check with him and make him aware that his method of seeking help was wrong and that he would be held accountable for such transgression.

After some enquiries, it was confirmed that the senior police constable did not need to be transferred out and could remain working in the same district until his retirement.

Connie's reflection

At the time of handling the incident, I considered that my life was not in danger. Thus, I approached the senior police constable and lowered myself at a close distance from him. However, after thinking carefully in hindsight, in the future I should treat every situation where firearms or lethal weapons are involved with great caution. I should maintain a safe distance between myself and an armed person.

When I joined the police force in 1988 at inspectorate rank, female police officers were not trained to carry firearms. Since 1995, all female police officers joining the police force are fully trained in firearm use and carry them while on duty. Female officers like me, who joined before 1995, were given a choice with respect to training in the use of firearms. I still remember the day that I signed the consent form. I was one of many female officers to choose to carry firearms.

To this day, I still feel it was the right decision. Why? I learnt how to use a service revolver and received regular training every quarter. Part of the training simulates responding to dangerous scenarios. This enhances the ability of police officers to make split-second decisions in emergency situations.

One might speculate as to whether the senior police constable really intended to shoot himself. The difficulty he faced seemed minor, and his actions seemed very much disproportionate. Were his actions simply a theatrical show, performed in order to have his superiors acquiesce to his wish to not be transferred? I did not pursue the police constable on this matter. The truth is I had no desire to find out the answer.

What may seem to be minor issues to a rational person may be overwhelming to the distressed person, and the problem could seemingly be irresolvable. Each individual's resilience in handling difficult situations is different. When the person confides her/his troubles in you, it may be more helpful to empathise with her/his situation without being judgemental.

Connie's note

This story was first published in an official journal, *Imprint* 18, The Annual Anthology of Women in Publishing Society Hong Kong, in 2019.

Cordon

The floor where my office was situated housed a general registry, as well as the offices of patrol subunits and others. It was a busy floor. Cordoning the whole corridor and confining personnel in their offices essentially isolated the environment. With no unnecessary or unplanned intrusions, the senior inspector and I were able to give our full attention to the crisis at hand.

Part C:

THE SECOND C— COMMAND

Chapter Seven

An Unusual Way to End a Negotiation (Barricade)

Crisis negotiator Edwin Lui

Dating, courtship, and falling in love can be so exciting and energising. Mutual feelings connect. The spirit soars. It is a fantastic journey. However, not every love story has a fairy-tale ending.

There is no best way to end a relationship when one or both parties feel that it is not working out. In this scenario, a man refuses to accept the breakup. He demands to see his girlfriend and threatens harm to her mother. While a negotiator talks to the man, a third party brings the negotiation to an end—somewhat unexpectedly.

On an early summer evening in 2001, a woman was on her way home. Upon reaching the ground floor lobby, she saw her daughter's ex-boyfriend, who insisted on following her up to the flat. He became frustrated when he found out that his ex-girlfriend was not at home, and he flew into a rage.

'I love her so much! I can't bear to lose her. She can't just leave me like that. Tell her to come here and tell me face to face why she is leaving me! I must see her now! Tell me where is she? She can't hide from me forever.' The man kept talking and shouting incessantly.

The girlfriend's mother said timidly, 'Please listen to me. She is not at home. I don't know when she will be back. There is no point hanging around like this. You two have broken up, so—'

The man cut her short with a wave of his hand. He walked from one end of the living room to the other. There was not much space, so he had to make a turn every three to four steps.

The woman's legs felt like jelly, so she said no more and tried to appear composed. The mother had previously witnessed the man's sudden outburst of temper when he and her daughter had paid a visit to her home. Recently, her daughter had moved back to Hong Kong for good, after finishing her studies. She had broken up with her boyfriend.

The woman managed to call the police. When uniformed police officers arrived, they noticed the iron gate and the wooden door were left ajar. Upon hearing the sound of a police beat radio, a man spoke through the doors. 'Yes, this is the right place. Come on in!'

A man in his twenties was sitting on a sofa beside the woman. He was grasping the woman's shoulder firmly with his left hand, and his right hand held a knife against her neck. The police cordoned off the area and requested the assistance of the Police Negotiation Cadre (PNC).

Edwin Lui joined the PNC in 1999 and remained a member until his retirement in 2012. He was a senior inspector of police at the time of handling the incident. He attended the scene with his PNC team and assumed the role of negotiator. The man talked about his upbringing, his study, and how he came to know his girlfriend. He had only one demand: he insisted on seeing his girlfriend face to face.

'How could you call that a break-up, huh? She just sent me a text message. Look at this. She said we need to take a break and that I deserved someone better. She refused to see me. That was it. How could she treat me like that? What have I done to deserve such treatment?' The man spoke angrily. He was full of resentment and was prone to outbursts. The man lived and studied overseas. He had met the woman's daughter at the university they had both attended. They had dated for some time.

As they talked, the man asked edgily, 'Who is this guy walking in and out?' The police incident commander had walked into the flat on a few occasions to check on the progress of the negotiation. The negotiator explained the incident commander's identity and role and reassured the man that no one was going to harm him or force him to do anything.

In time, the man became calmer. He removed the knife from the proximity of the woman's neck and placed it on his lap. He paid minimal attention to the incident commander's occasional appearance.

In the midst of the negotiation, the incident commander, without warning, lunged forward. He performed a few swift manoeuvres and succeeded in pinning the man to the ground, while at the same time kicking the knife out of his hand. Immediately, officers of the tactical team rushed in and handcuffed the man. Edwin looked on in wonder. He thought that given the commander's coordination of his arms and legs, he appeared to have had training in the use of martial arts.

When the man was brought to his feet, he looked defeated and was in tears. The negotiator said to the man in a caring tone, 'Young man, I understand you love that girl. It is a harrowing experience to lose the love of your life, but if it is not working out, you can't force her to come back to you. Love has to be mutual. Shouting and making threats will not solve any problem.' As he was led away by the uniformed police officers, the man neither looked at the negotiator nor said anything. The negotiator hoped that the man might give some consideration to what he had said.

Edwin Lui's reflection

Edwin still had a vivid memory of the incident because of the way that the crisis was brought to an end. The incident commander's unannounced appearance in the vicinity where he and the man were talking distracted the man's attention at times. Nevertheless, Edwin managed to calm the man and got him to refocus on their ongoing conversation.

The commander's sudden action caught him off guard at the time. Reflecting upon the incident later, Edwin appreciated the incident from a police officer's point of view. The incident commander took a decisive action at a moment that he/she saw was the right time to act. For the element of surprise to be effective, it was understandable from the point of view of the incident commander not to inform anyone, including the negotiator. The tactical team rushed to the assistance of the commander. The woman was rescued unharmed, and the culprit was apprehended. The incident commander did succeed in resolving the crisis peacefully with no casualty. Therefore, he felt there was no right or wrong in such a decision.

Command

Gilbert Wong, co-author, is of the view that the case demonstrated police officers' lean towards an action imperative mode from an operational perspective. The incident commander in this case had personally monitored the progress of the negotiation. Apparently, the commander needed to see in his own eyes the build of the man, the mood of the talk, and the progressing atmosphere in order to look for a golden opportunity to carry out his plan. Did the commander have this planned out from the beginning, or did he spring into action once he saw a chance to do so? Either one could be the case. Moreover, the tactical team reinforced the commander immediately, and the rescue operation was a success. An incident commander personally taking action like this is not the norm. Gilbert can say confidently that not many people in the Hong Kong police have such good martial arts skills as that guy.

Gilbert has, in his twenty-two years' experience as a member of the PNC, witnessed gradual changes in the working relationship between the regular police officers, the PNC team, and the tactical team. All parties appreciate the importance and value of a triangular working framework when dealing with a crisis.

Chapter Eight

Judgement Call (Barricade)

Crisis negotiators Edwin Lui and Gilbert Wong

Can you judge silence? Does silence always convey a sense of peacefulness? Can silence be threatening? A police negotiator tries talking to an armed man who has barricaded himself inside a public housing flat. The negotiator talks to him through closed doors. The man does not respond. Is it a one-sided or two-way communication? What are the alternatives?

On a day in mid-2003, a police constable paid a visit to a man's home with a view to execute a warrant of arrest. Why was the man subject to an arrest warrant? Some time ago, he had failed to switch on his headlight when he was cycling along a cycling track at night in the New Territories. A police constable intercepted him and issued him with a summons for contravening the relevant traffic regulation. However, the man failed to attend the court to answer the summons. Consequently, the magistrate issued a warrant of arrest to bring him to court to answer the summons.

The police constable pressed the doorbell of the flat, where the man lived. The man opened the door. Upon learning of the purpose of the constable's visit, the man tore up the court document, punched the police constable, and flashed a knife at him. The man then closed the door. The police constable called for reinforcements.

Gilbert Wong and Edwin Lui joined the PNC in 1999. They were senior inspectors of police at the time of handling this incident. They and their PNC team attended the scene. The tactical team, the emergency unit of the New Territories south region, had already arrived and guarding the scene.

Edwin, the negotiator, initiated a dialogue. 'Hey, man, I am here to offer you help. I am aware that an incident had occurred. Would you like to tell me what happened?' The man did not respond. Edwin decided to state facts. 'I am aware that a police officer tried to issue you a summons earlier on. The summons is issued by the court, not by the police. The police officer is only carrying out the court's order. Besides, the traffic offence you have committed is very minor. The sentence is usually only a few hundred dollars' fine. If you have financial difficulty paying the fine, you can apply to the court to reduce the amount.'

After a while, the man mumbled in a low voice, 'The government bullies people. They bully poor people like me.' There was a pause.

'Are you living with someone?'

'Only me here. They all left. Let them be. Like I care,' he scoffed.

'Uh huh. I see, you have a bike. Do you like cycling?'

'Um, it's an old bike. Someone threw it out. I did some repair here and there, and then it worked. Riding to places, the market, was not bad and quite convenient.' Other than these sporadic statements, the man basically kept to himself and refused to engage in further talk.

Gilbert swapped with Edwin to talk to the man. After a brief introduction, he said, 'I have a suggestion. You open the wooden door, but keep the iron gate closed. I can see you. You can see me.' There was no response. 'How about you let me in? I have no weapon. I'm just going to come in alone.' No response.

'What I understand is this ...'Gilbert proceeded to describe the sequence of events, according to the account provided by the uniformed police officer. He varied the tone and speed of his speech: sometimes loud, sometimes soft, sometimes faster, sometimes slower. There was a pause.

A uniformed police officer had identified an observation point, where, from time to time, he could see the man's movement through a window in his flat. He reported what he saw to the incident commander and the PNC team. Sometimes the man would enter the kitchen. Sometimes he would stand behind the wooden door, trying to figure out what was happening outside. Nearly an hour had passed.

At the request of the police, the gas company had switched off the main gas supply to the whole building. This was a precautionary measure, in case the man tampered with the gas pipe in his flat and endangered other residents.

There was no positive progress in the negotiation. There was also a growing concern about what the man might be up to. He might be doing nothing, or he might be preparing for combat. At length, the police incident commander said, 'Inform EU to get ready to break down the doors. We will make a forced entry.'

The tactical team members were dressed in full tactical suits. They carried armadillo shields, batons, firearms, door rams, hammers, crowbars, and the like. They approached the man's flat, which was situated at the end of a long corridor. At approximately 7.20 in the evening, the officers cut open the iron gate first and broke down the wooden door. Next, everything happened very quickly.

A picture of a long corridor with flats on both sides in
a public housing building, similar to this scenario.

Edwin and Gilbert witnessed pandemonium break loose. The
man wielded knives and attacked the police officers. The officers raised their shields to take the blunt force of the knives.
They tried to push the man to a corner in the toilet. The man
had knives placed at different places in his home, including the
toilet. They also tried to subdue the man by spraying OC foam
onto his face. However, one police officer fell down because
the OC foam caused the floor to become slippery. Other police
officers frantically tried to protect him. The scene resembled
a battlefield. There was shouting, yelling, and groaning. After
some minutes, the man was eventually subdued.

A staged photograph of a tactical team in tactical gear
and breaking down a door with a door ram.

Reflection by Edwin and Gilbert

The police negotiators watched in consternation as they saw injured colleagues being helped out of the flat, one after another.
The man had wounded four police officers in the violent scuffle,
one rather gravely. The man himself sustained minor injury.

After the man was subdued, it was revealed that he had carried
two knives on his body. He had also planted knives at different
places in his flat, including at the toilet. The fact that he had
placed so many knives inside his flat strongly indicated that he
was not going to surrender peacefully.

The case was one of the most difficult situations that the negotiators had handled. Given that the man was unresponsive
and the closed doors blocked all communication, they had to

maintain a dialogue in hopes to trigger a response. The incident commander had a difficult decision to make regarding the way forward.

Command

What are the factors, which affect decision making? The police incident commander had to consider a number of diverse factors in this particular situation. Other than divulging a little bit about himself, the man basically remained unresponsive. The negotiation was at a stalemate. The manpower availability had to be taken into consideration. It was difficult to estimate the probable danger that might lie ahead. The unease in the neighbourhood might escalate if the situation could not be brought under control. The PNC team played an advisory role. The incident commander made the final decision.

It is easier said than done when talking in hindsight. It is not an easy decision to make. It is a judgement call.

Could the police have waited outside the flat and let the man come out in his own time? The man had disobeyed a warrant of arrest, torn up a court document, and assaulted a police officer. The police had waited nearly three hours. No one knew what the man was up to inside the flat. He was acting irrationally and was armed. Could the police have waited for the man to come out? Such questions can be debated, but that rarely results in consensus, even amongst experts.

Chapter Nine

Hanging on to Ting Kau Bridge (Attempted Suicide)

Crisis negotiators Sindy Chan and Wilbut Chan

Modern bridges, especially those that link land masses above expanses of seabed, are showcases of architectural and technological excellence. Unfortunately, some have also become favoured locations for those people who are intent on committing suicide. The Ting Kau Bridge in Hong Kong has, from time to time, been the site of such attempts at suicide.

Ting Kau Bridge is a 1,777-metres, cable-stayed vehicular bridge that connects west and north-west New Territories to the urban area. In some parts where it links land masses and seabed, the height is elevated up to sixty-two meters above the ground or sea level (The Highways Department, the Government of the Hong Kong Special Administrative Region, *Ting Kau Bridge and Approach Viaduct*).

In the early hours of a morning in the last quarter of 2008, a woman in her mid-forties hailed a taxi to take her to Ting Kau Bridge. At the midsection of the bridge, she threatened to jump out of the moving cab if the driver would not stop. Reluctantly, the taxi driver stopped to let out the woman. She appeared to be quite drunk. The taxi driver decided to make a report to police.

Wilbut Chan joined the PNC in 1999. He was one of the four regional coordinators of the PNC. He was a superintendent at the time of handling the incident. On that night, he was on overnight shift duty as the duty controller at the regional command and control centre, New Territories (RCCC NT). RCCC NT is one of the four centres in the Hong Kong police force which takes emergency 999 calls.

As a duty controller, he was the highest in command at the RCCC NT. He obtained firsthand information of the case, and at the request of the police at the scene, he called his PNC team member. His team was the on-call team on that particular day. Wilbut would contact his team members to attend the scene first. Once he was off the night shift duty at seven in the morning, he would also attend the scene to help his PNC teammates.

Sindy Chan was sound asleep. Her mobile phone rang and woke her up.

'Hello, Sindy, can you assist?' The caller was a male. His voice sounded formal and urgent. He did not identify who he was.

She looked at her clock: it was just after four thirty in the morning. A thought came to Sindy's mind. It must be someone very desperate to borrow money. 'To help what?' she replied in a sleepy tone.

'A woman has climbed over the fence of the Ting Kau Bridge to attempt suicide. Can you go to the scene?'

'Who are—Oh! You are Wilbut, my team leader! Oh! Sorry, yes, yes, I'll be on my way. Where is the location again?' Sindy was fully awake by then. She dressed quickly, went downstairs, and hailed a taxi.

Sindy Chan joined the PNC in 2001. She was a sergeant at the time of handling this incident. When the taxi arrived at a mid-section of the Ting Kau Bridge, police vehicles and fire services vehicles were parked there.

'Stop behind the police vehicles, please,' Sindy told the taxi driver.

'Miss, the whole bridge is a no-stopping zone!'

Sindy showed her police warrant card to the driver; no more explanation was required. He stopped the taxi, took the fare, and drove off. *The taxi driver would not be able to pick up any other passenger for the rest of the journey along the bridge, and he probably had to drive back without passenger too. Poor guy,* Sindy thought with a sigh.

At five thirty in the morning, darkness was beginning to fade. Sindy had just returned from an overseas training course in crisis negotiation, organised by the Federal Bureau of Investigation (FBI) in September 2008. In the training, she learned that the Golden Gate Bridge in San Francisco, California, was infamous for its high incidence of suicide attempts. Upon seeing where the woman was, Sindy was concerned that they might not have sufficient time to save her. She did not hold out much hope of a successful outcome.

The woman was sitting on the far end of the horizontal arm of what appeared to be a metal anemometer, which extended outwards from the bridge. To reach there, the woman had to climb over a fence of the bridge one and a half meters in height, cross a two-metre-wide platform, and then walk or crawl the entire length of the horizontal rod to its tip. The total length of the horizontal arm measured around seven metres long. The woman was wearing a flowery dress and a pair of slippers. From her slurred speech, she appeared to be heavily intoxicated and thus oblivious to the danger.

A picture of a section of Ting Kau Bridge where a woman attempted suicide. The black arrow indicates the location of the distraught woman. Police negotiators, uniformed police officers, and paramedics were at the scene. Courtesy of *Sing Tao Daily*, Hong Kong.

A picture of a team of crisis negotiators communicating with a suicidal woman at Ting Kau Bridge. Sindy (first one from the right) was handling the crisis. Courtesy of *Sing Tao Daily*, Hong Kong.

'Hello, miss. I see that you are depressed. I'm here to offer you help and listen to you. You are not alone. What has caused you to be so unhappy?' Sindy shouted at the top of her voice. Later, she had recourse to a loudhailer.

Sindy had to strain her ears to hear what the woman said because no equipment could be provided to her. At first, the woman talked nonsensically. 'I'm fine, no need to worry. I'm feeling happy. You are such a nice person, listening and talking to me. It is my own decision to choose this path. I will be responsible for my action. I won't blame you.' She laughed sporadically. Her intoxication had impaired her thought processes. She was consuming beer, one can after another.

In between, she talked about her family. About a week or so ago, her eldest son, whom she loved very much, had passed away as a result of illness. She lived with her younger son, but he was not that close to her. The younger son felt that his mother spent all her time taking care of his sick, elder brother. Recently, the woman broke up with her boyfriend because she found out that he was married. However, she missed him a lot and tried to call him. She felt more heartbroken when he did not answer her calls.

Meanwhile, Wilbut Chan finished work and arrived at the scene to relieve Sindy's negotiator role. Sindy proceeded to discuss the situation with the fire services personnel. They did not know the strength of the anemometer arm, so it was hazardous to step onto the metal frame to reach the woman. To allow her to fall and rescue her from the sea was too dangerous an option to consider. After careful consideration, the firemen formulated a plan.

Suddenly, the woman moved farther outwards. She was then sitting on a single metal rod. She rested one hand on a vertical rod, the farthest point. She even stood up. She did this several times, apparently to ease the numbness in her legs, after they had been dangling in the air for some time. Then she started throwing items away: her bag, the knife, and lastly the slippers from her feet. 'I'm going to see my son,' she said. The PNC team sensed the woman's behaviour did not bode well.

Wilbut paced himself and spoke to the woman through the loudhailer. 'You keep saying that you are going to see your elder son. Do you know your elder son is watching you now, from above? He is counting on you to take care of his younger brother. Seeing you give up on yourself like this, he is distraught and worried about you. Feel his presence. He is telling you not to give up on yourself. He is telling you to take care of his younger brother. He loves you very much. Your younger son needs you. You have been so brave to face all your troubles on your own. Your elder son is giving you support from above. You are not alone. Can you feel the sun's warmth on your body? A fresh day brings new hope.'

As Wilbut continued the encouraging talk, the firemen were getting ready to use a fire engine, which was equipped with a hydraulic platform and rescue cage. The biggest concern was the carrying weight of the turntable ladder. It was designed for extending upwards to conduct a rescue. In this scenario, the turntable ladder with the cage had to be stretched horizontally outwards. The weight of the cage might cause the fire engine to tip and topple. However, there was no other way, and time was running out. They had to make an attempt.

The turntable ladder carrying the fireman in the cage extended outwards at around a forty-five-degree angle, trying to reach the woman. Sindy saw the woman recoil in fear and said, 'Hey, wait a minute, the noise of the engine and the approach route at high angle probably look rather intimidating to the woman. She might fall any time if she keeps moving like this.' The firemen retrieved the turntable ladder and started over again. This time, the turntable ladder moved outwards and almost parallel to the horizontal rod towards the woman. The fireman carried a police beat radio to maintain communication with the negotiator.

When the fireman reached the woman, he spoke calmly, just as Wilbut had instructed him to do so, through the police beat radio. 'Come, miss, let me hold you. Do not be afraid. You will be safe with me.' The woman did not resist. The fireman put a safety harness around her body and let her step on the outer edge of the cage. Any major movement, such as climbing over the fence to get into the cage, might result in a violent jerking of both the ladder and the cage. The risk of the fire engine toppling would be exacerbated. The combined effort of those professionals resulted in the safe rescue of the woman.

'Miss, you have done very well in allowing the fireman to take you to safety. It is not easy to take that brave step. Remember, your elder son is counting on you to look after your younger son. Take good care of yourself.' Sindy comforted the woman as she was escorted to an ambulance. The woman was weak but otherwise unharmed.

Sindy's and Wilbut's reflections

So many factors could have caused the rescue operation to fail. The woman's heavy intoxication impaired her ability to make rational judgements and at the same time emboldened her to have made that perilous journey. Whilst in that state, she had entrapped herself in abandonment and a false sense of peace. The woman might fall anytime by accident or a flash decision.

The only mode of communication between the negotiators and the woman was through the loudhailer. The mechanical sound quality coming out from a loudhailer diminished the warmth of a human voice to a large extent. They were seven metres apart, so it was difficult for the negotiators to maintain any eye contact or use body language to project care and concern.

As traffic picked up along the bridge on an adjacent lane, the rumbling sound of the heavy trucks made it even harder for the negotiators to hear the woman talk.

When the rescue plan began, Sindy noticed the woman recoil in fear as the cage carrying the fireman approached. She sensed that the woman might be alarmed by the noise caused by the moving turntable ladder and the cage bearing down on the woman at a high angle. If she was not able to remain calm, the woman might fall by accident any minute. Sindy immediately informed the fire services to retreat and try another way of approaching. They tried again by moving the ladder at almost parallel angle with the metal rod where the woman was sitting. They attributed the successful rescue to effective command and coordination—and luck.

Command

The PNC, the uniformed police officers handling the case, the firemen, and last but not the least the woman played their important roles in this scenario. Thanks to the negotiator's active listening and endearing talk, the woman felt a glimpse of hope and changed her mind. Without her willingness to cooperate, the fireman would not have been able to put a harness around her and bring her to safety.

The fire services, the PNC team, and the police battled against time and adapted the rescue plan in light of the changing circumstances. To reiterate, effective command, timely coordination, and luck saved a life.

Chapter Ten

Tribute to a fireman
(Attempted Suicide)

Crisis negotiator Wilbut Chan

A man has set a deadline: he would jump at six thirty. He has no watch. There is no need for one. 'Do-do-do-do ...' the musical tune announcing the six thirty evening news coming from the neighbourhood's televisions would be the signal which would precipitate his death leap. The firemen and the police negotiators were determined to save him and did just that, albeit against his wishes.

On an autumn afternoon in 2003, the police received a 999 call for help. Uniformed police officers arrived at the door of a residential unit in the New Territories. An elderly woman in her late seventies was lying on the floor. Her white hair was stained red from the blood still oozing from her scalp. She was rushed to hospital in an unconscious state.

At the same time, an elderly man in his eighties had climbed out of the flat through a window and was sitting on a ledge on the outer wall of the building, many floors above the ground. The Police Negotiation Cadre (PNC) was called to attend the scene.

Wilbut Chan joined the PNC in 1999. He was a senior inspector at the time of handling this incident. The incident occurred in the police division where he worked. He and the police incident commander rushed to the scene. Other PNC members came to his assistance shortly after.

Wilbut walked on the bloodied floor to reach the window. The man responded calmly to the negotiator's questions.

'We had an early dinner as usual. Out of nowhere, she talked about my unruly young days. I was young. I did things that hurt her feelings, but I thought that she had forgiven me. She would not stop talking. Anger was boiling inside me. That thing on the floor, I bashed her head with it. That stopped her from talking. I will go to jail. At my age, I probably won't be coming out alive.'

Wilbut listened patiently and did not pass any judgement. He learned that the couple had several children. A son lived with them, and others had moved out. *There ought to be something in the man's mind that was holding him from taking the ultimate plunge*, the negotiator thought. The PNC team would try to find out what the man valued in his life.

'Can I contact your son?' asked Wilbut.

'He hates me. He never calls me Papa.'

'What makes you think that he hates you? What does he call you?'

'He calls me scumbag! When it is time for the meal, he says, Scumbag, mealtime, come out. That's how he calls me,' the man replied in a seemingly indifferent tone. He stayed home most of the time. He had no money to spare. He did not like socialising with his neighbours, in any case. He would take a walk in the playground nearby occasionally. That was all.

Meanwhile, a man and woman arrived at the flat. They were the couple's children. 'How is our father? Has he jumped?' they both enquired anxiously.

'Your father is not hurt. Can you provide some information about him? We need your assistance,' a PNC member replied. He thought that it was a positive sign that the man's children had shown up.

After some hesitation, one of them replied, 'We just need to know whether he had jumped. Since he is still alive, we will leave now.'

'Why do you need to leave now? We need your assistance. Your father's situation is still very dangerous. He may jump at any time.'

'It's OK if he is still alive. We need to leave now. If he jumps and we are around, the reporters might find out our relationship with him. We don't want to have any association with him,' one replied. The other nodded in agreement, and then they left.

The PNC team members were baffled as to why the children behaved so cold-heartedly. In any case, they decided not to disclose the children's presence to the man. The negotiator asked the man about his other children. The man did not know about the two children's hasty appearance and made no mention of them. He indicated that another son, his daughter-in-law, and his grandson lived overseas.

One PNC team member dialled the overseas number provided by the man, using the PNC member's own phone. The son answered the call. After having heard what was happening to his father, he replied, 'He hasn't jumped? That's fine, then. My family is having dinner.'

'Your father might jump any time. The situation is dire,' the PNC member said earnestly.

'He hasn't jumped. Then things are still OK. We are having dinner. Please call later, after we finish our meal. Bye.' The son's tone was disarmingly normal, without the slightest hint of concern. To him, the phone call was an unwelcome intrusion into his and his family's life.

By then, it became apparent to the PNC team that the elderly man lived a miserable and lonely life.

'What is the time now?' the elderly man asked.

'Can you tell me why you wish to know the time?' Wilbut did not feel good about the man's question. From experience, he knew that a suicidal person asking about the time was cause for alarm, because it indicated that he/she might have a definite time frame with respect to his/her suicide.

'Half past six is the time that I will jump.'

'I will definitely not tell you the time,' responded the negotiator.

'It's not a problem. At six thirty, I shall hear the "do-do-do" sound from the neighbourhood's televisions. Everyone switches on their TV to listen to the evening news. I'll hear "do-do-do" everywhere. Then I'll jump. Don't you worry,' the man said calmly.

The PNC team and the firemen did not doubt that the man meant what he said. Without the man's cooperation, it would be near impossible to conduct a high-angle rescue. The firemen came up with a plan.

'Are you OK to do this? It is not without risk,' the officer in charge of the fire services asked his subordinate, a fireman of slender build.

'Yes, sir. I want to try. I should be OK,' the fireman replied without hesitation. He proceeded to take off his tunic and harness.

His colleagues tied a rope around his waist and secured the other end of the line.

Half past six was only a minute away. In a spectacular feat of derring-do, the fireman sprinted forward, jumped through the window and caught hold of the man. In that same instance, firemen descended from the floor above and secured the pair. The team of firemen managed to rescue the man and bring him back into the flat.

His colleagues quickly untied the rope around the fireman, who had virtually jumped out of the window in order to catch the old man. The sudden descent of the two people was arrested by a violent jerk of the rope tied around the fireman's waist. One particular area on his trunk had taken the combined weight of two people, plus the pull of gravity.

'Sir, the fireman performed a heroic act to save you. Your family members worry about you. Please take good care of yourself.' said Wilbut.

'My wife is likely to survive the attack. None of my children cares about me. I have no friends, no money. I'll go to jail. What is there to live for? You should not have saved me. I'll jump again.' The man's bitter reply dampened the spirits of his rescuers. He maintained the same glassy stare and resolve no matter what the PNC members said.

Eventually, the PNC members fell silent and held each other in mutual support. The uniformed police officers arrested the old man for having assaulted his wife and took him into custody.

Wilbut's reflection

Wilbut and his PNC team tried talking about a range of topics to find something that the elderly man might value in life. They could not understand the indifference of the man's two children, who turned up at the scene, or the attitude of the other son living overseas. They must had found out about their father's assault on their mother. One might well expect that the children would show great concern for their mother while displaying anger towards the father. However, Wilbut saw no sign of such reactions. All of the children were indifferent to what had transpired. What had happened that had led to such an irreparable rift between the man and his children? Wilbut could not find any clue throughout the negotiation.

The lack of progress and the time frame set by the man put everyone under great pressure. After much deliberation, the fire services commander decided to conduct the rescue operation, without the consent of the man.

Wilbut stood in awe of the fireman who had volunteered to take on the crucial role in the rescue operation. The fire services commander had to choose a fireman of slim build to do the job. The reason for this was that the narrow window frame was too small to allow a fireman of more pronounced build, in full protective gear, to jump through. If the firemen started pulling apart the window frame structure, the man would sense their plan right away and would have jumped.

No one could be certain whether the firemen's plan was going to work. If the elderly man had struggled violently during the rescue, the three firemen could have been pulled down together. This could well have had a fatal outcome. Timing and coordination was pivotal in the successful rescue of the old man. It was a one-take shot.

So many people had worked to save the elderly man. They should be clapping hands and congratulating each other for having done such an excellent job. How could the man say such words? He did not show any gratitude for what was an exceptional act of bravery. Not only that, but he vowed that he would jump again. Everything they had done counted for nought. In that instant, the team's initial feeling of euphoria dissipated.

Instead of feeling relief, the PNC team tried talking to the man, imploring him to treasure his life. His complete lack of responsiveness was a blow to everyone's spirit.

Before they left, Wilbut and his teammates held each other for some minutes, to regain their composure. The uniformed police officers and the firemen were also emotionally affected by the elderly man's reply.

The PNC team held an operational debriefing shortly afterwards. It was important to acknowledge each other's good work and reinforce the notion that the elderly man was ultimately responsible for the choice, which he had made, and for whatever action he might undertake in the future.

Over the next few days, Wilbut avoided reading the local news reports. He would rather not know about the elderly man's demise if indeed he had succeeded in killing himself. Wilbut carried a heavy, emotional burden for some time before he could let go of the matter.

Command

In such a situation, the officer in charge of the fire services is the overall commander in the rescue operation. He has the sole authority to decide how and when the rescue operation is to be carried out.

The police incident commander, the PNC team, and the firemen worked hand in hand, in constructing a plan to rescue the old man. The progress of the negotiation was conveyed to the decision maker, who then made the final decision to commence the rescue operation.

Part D:

THE THIRD C— COMMUNICATION

Chapter Eleven

Using a Negotiation Throw-Ball (Barricade)

Crisis negotiator Arie Chan

In this situation, a negotiation throw-ball was used to establish communication with a person who held his family members captive and refused to surrender himself to police. The lifespan of the use of the negotiation throw-ball was unexpectedly cut short. Nevertheless, the crisis was resolved without any casualties after nearly six hours of negotiation.

Arie Chan joined the Police Negotiation cadre (PNC) in 2004. On a late evening in 2007, Arie was called upon to assist in the resolution of a crisis. A man in his late forties had barged into the home of his ex-wife. He had barricaded himself, his ex-wife, and their three children inside a public housing unit in Kowloon. Unable to reach an agreement about the custody of the children, he threatened them with a chopper and locked the doors. His wife managed to dial 999 to call the police. The three children hid inside their bedroom, but the flimsy door could not be locked. Not long after their arrival, the police picked up a piece of paper that landed on the ground floor. It read, 'Help! Help! Rescue us, please.' The police looked up and saw the three young kids at a window, many floors above ground level.

Arie and her PNC team of five to six members arrived outside the flat. The wooden door and the iron gate were closed. There was a small ventilation window beside the door. The window's horizontal glass panes were locked, and the curtain was drawn.

A picture depicting an entrance of a public housing flat. The setting of an iron gate, wooden door, and ventilation window is similar to this scenario.

Arie took up the role of negotiator. 'Hello, mister, I am a police negotiator. I have come to offer you help. Can you open the door? You only need to open the wooden door. You can keep the iron gate locked. I won't come in without your permission.' There was no response from the man, and no sound could be heard. The negotiator tried different ways to initiate a dialogue, but to no avail.

The man had a history of violence towards his ex-wife. There was real concern that the man might assault his ex-wife and the children.

The police incident commander had briefed the tactical team about the situation. He told members of the team to be ready to make a forced entry, on his command. The fire services personnel had taken up a position, from where they could conduct a high-angle rescue from the floors above. Contingency rescue plans were formulated in preparation for a worst-case scenario. The PNC informed the incident commander that they would use their equipment, a negotiation throw-ball, to facilitate communication. A tenant of a flat directly above the man's flat had kindly provided his home as a working station for the negotiator and her team members.

A PNC member held one end of the attaching cable and lowered the ball through the window of the upper floor flat and along the outer wall of the building, to reach the level of the man's unit.

'A bit lower... yes, the level is good. Steady. Okay, now turn the ball a bit to your right. This position is good, I can see a bit of the living room through the lens.' A PNC team member talked with Arie as he adjusted the angle of the ball.

'OK, we are all set. Arie, take this, and you can talk to the man.' A PNC team member informed Arie and handed the microphone over to her.

Arie had gone up to the upper floor flat and took over the microphone. She began, 'Hey, man, how are you? How are your kids? I wish to talk to you. I am on an upper floor flat. I have lowered a round device outside your window. Look outside. You should be able to see it.'

'What? What is that? Do you want to film me? F--- off! Go away. I won't talk to anybody. Go away!' The man reacted angrily and repeatedly swore at the negotiator.

'Guy, listen to me. Listen here. This thing is an electronic device for communication. It has no recording function. With the help of this device, you can hear my voice when I talk. I can also hear you speak. I am here to offer you help.' The negotiator spoke calmly and at an even pace. Then she paused and waited for the man's response. The combined weight of the ball and the cable was quite heavy. The PNC team members had to take turns holding the cable, to keep the ball steady.

Suddenly, the ball's screen monitor showed a dark shadow. Not long after, there were raised voices emanating from the uniformed police officers on the ground floor, 'The man is chopping at the ball! He is trying to cut off the attaching cable!' To prevent further damage, the PNC team retrieved the ball.

It was obvious that the man was still in a defensive mode. Arie returned to her original position outside the man's flat and began talking to the man again, 'OK, I see that you don't like the idea of the ball. I want you to feel comfortable talking to me. I'll station myself outside the door of your flat. How are your kids? You want custody of your children, don't you? They are scared of their papa when you behave like this.'

'I did not hurt my kids. I don't care that the woman leaves me, but she can't snatch the kids away from me! I want my kids back! My kids back!' the man shouted repeatedly. Arie listened patiently and acknowledged the man's feelings as he vented his anger and grievances. She noticed that the man directed his anger solely towards his wife. There was a perceptible tone of gentleness when he talked about his children.

While the man's attention was distracted, the ex-wife had quietly walked to the balcony and climbed over the fence to reach an adjacent unit. The firemen positioned on the outer wall of the building above spotted her right away and helped her to safety. The man heard the commotion but was too late to stop his ex-wife's escape. He shouted and swore repeatedly. Then he stopped.

After a period of silence, Arie said, 'Your kids matter a lot to you. No matter what happens, you are still their father. Nobody can take that away from you. I can refer you to a social worker. They can assist you to initiate contact with your ex-wife so you can talk about the custody of your children and have access to them. There are options. It doesn't have to be this way. Why don't you open the door, and we can talk more on your concerns?'

In time, the man's stance softened. Eventually, he opened the door to let the police enter the flat. The children were shaken but not harmed. The negotiation concluded after 2.00 a.m. in the morning. It had taken six hours.

Arie's reflection

During that night, the uniformed police officers, the fire services, and the PNC team had to request access to several flats to monitor the situation, conduct the negotiation, and prepare for rescue action. All the talk, noise, and action had disrupted the peace and quiet of the neighbourhood for many hours into the night. Arie felt very grateful for their generosity and patience. The operation would have faced any number of other obstacles without their help.

Arie used the throw-ball to facilitate communication. The sound quality was satisfactory both ways. It was quite an effort for her team members to hold the throw-ball for a prolonged period, because it was quite heavy. Unfortunately, the man tried to damage the equipment, and it had to be retrieved.

Communication

This case exhibited the importance of effective communication. The man had closed the doors to his flat and refused to talk to the negotiators. They tried to establish communication through a negotiation throw-ball, but it could not be used due to the man's objection. Nevertheless, Arie continued to engage the man in active listening. In time, the man softened his hostile stance, came to his senses, and surrendered.

Chapter Twelve

Triangular Relationship (Attempted Suicide)

Crisis negotiators Gilbert Wong and Elizabeth Ma

Imagine yourself watching an episode on television. In the flash of an eye, you can become completely absorbed in what is transpiring on the screen. Before you know it, the screen turns black, and there is only a distant, muffled, cracking sound. Then nothing. This is an apt comparison of what may happen during a suicide-related crisis. A person may be so intent on dying that the fatal jump could happen any second, without warning. It is the role of the police negotiator to stabilise a situation so the fatal decision does not come to pass.

In this case, the negotiator manages to preserve two hours of a woman's life. However, nothing seems to matter to her. They are about to lose her at any time.

What made that woman, who seemed so determined to die, change her mind? What pushed her to such desperation in the first place?

On a summer afternoon, a young woman was standing barefoot on a thin, metal railing on the rooftop of a thirty-storey building in the New Territories. Without hesitation, the attending uniformed police officers requested that the Police Negotiation Cadre (PNC) attend the scene to assist.

Gilbert Wong joined the PNC in 1999. He and two PNC team members arrived at the scene and assessed the background information, which the police had gathered from neighbours and other witnesses.

On that day, the woman was taking a stroll with her lover in a park. Both worked in a nearby restaurant, and they were on their usual afternoon break. The weather was fine. They were holding hands and talking affectionately. The woman's husband, who was supposed to be at work some miles away, turned up at the park and saw the pair. It was clear to the husband what was transpiring. He flew into a wild rage, swore at the couple, and punched the boyfriend. Only then did the boyfriend realise that the woman was married. Not daring to confront the husband, and to escape further harm, the boyfriend ran off.

Bewildered and shocked, the woman was left to take the full brunt of her husband's angst. A growing crowd of onlookers had gathered. She cried, screamed, and pleaded with her husband to stop. Some people tried to intervene. Suddenly, the woman dashed off into a nearby building.

Another woman was among the bystanders and was shouting hysterically. She had just found out that her husband was having an affair with the woman who had run off. These two couples, the woman and her husband and the woman's boyfriend and his wife, lived in the same public housing estate.

The woman had made her way to the rooftop of a thirty-storey building. When the PNC team located her, they saw that she was weeping pitifully. At the same time, she was talking to her mother on her mobile phone. 'Mom, please take good care of my daughter. Don't worry about me. I shall be fine. I'm OK.' She was telling her mother all the important dates and daily routines of her two-year-old daughter. She had left her shoes on the ground and stepped onto the top of a metal parapet. She placed one hand on a wall adjacent the parapet, which was half a person's height. That was the only anchor, and she held on to it.

From the negotiator's experience in handling jumping incidents, leaving one's shoes on the ground is a clear signal that the person has made up her/his mind to end her/his life.

Gilbert, the negotiator, listened patiently to the woman talking about her misery. She saw no way out of her loveless marriage, nor could she escape the ferocious temper of her husband. She was devastated by the fact that not only did her lover desert her, but he was also married. The relentless vilification by her husband in front of the neighbours destroyed any vestiges of dignity that still remained.

Though the two-year-old daughter mattered dearly to the woman, she seemed set upon putting her daughter under the care of her mother. It was clear that the woman was over-whelmed by feelings of utter hopelessness. On a number of occasions, it appeared as if she was making ready to release her grip on the wall. Gilbert shouted, 'Don't move!' The authoritative command succeeded in deterring the woman from jumping. But for how long?

The instant that she removed that hand, her life would be over. Two hours passed. That which was seemingly inevitable might happen at any time.

Gilbert made a rare decision to call a female police negotiator to assist in the crisis resolution. Elizabeth Ma arrived shortly afterwards and took over from Gilbert. What followed was not a miracle. It was attributed to Elizabeth's supportive demeanour and her skill and calmness in her communicative interactions with the woman.

She said to the woman, 'Dear girl, you are such a beautiful woman.' She paused so the words could sink in. Elizabeth paced herself as she continued. 'Have faith in yourself.' Another pause followed. A glimmer of hope could be seen in the woman's face.

'In the future, you will find someone who will treasure you and love you dearly.' Another pause followed. Elizabeth then slowly walked closer. 'Come down and let me hug you.' Elizabeth's comforting words reverberated in the atmosphere. In that defining moment, she helped the lady down and hugged her for all the time that she needed.

Gilbert's reflection

The gender of a negotiator in a crisis does not matter usually. However, the words of three male negotiators were ineffective in making the woman change her mind. After having talked to the woman for some time, Gilbert was more and more aware of the woman's steadfast determination to end her own life. The sense of hopelessness weighed heavily upon him. Gilbert decided to call Elizabeth to assist. He had always been aware and appreciative of the power of Elizabeth's caring demeanour and endearing voice.

Elizabeth's appearance transformed the whole situation. He remembered Elizabeth's words clearly. They were caring, simple, and to the point, and they reached the heart of the woman.

When Elizabeth was asked about this incident, she could not recall any details. That is quite normal because she had handled countless crises in her PNC career. Each negotiator's recollection of incidents may not be the same.

This incident was the not the first time that Gilbert saw a suicidal person take off his/her shoes at the jumping point. From his years of experience in handling similar jumping incidents, he noticed such a phenomenon in attempted and completed suicide cases. Very often, a suicidal person takes off his/her footwear and leaves them at the jumping point. Sometimes the person also leaves behind personal belongings, such as a purse or wristwatch. Gilbert has searched related literature about suicide and found no mention of the phenomenon.

Gilbert has explored possible explanations for this phenomenon with Dr Paul Wong. Did the person wish to leave an identifying sign, to let people know where he/she jumped? Did the person wish to leave some identifying details for people to track her/him down more easily? Or is there a simpler, less psychologically compelling reason for this practice? Might these objects be removed or left behind because they might prove to be obstacles or hindrances in the carrying out of the act of suicide? In any case, these two recognised authorities in this area of human behaviour could not reach consensus on the matter.

Communication

Gilbert often tells people that negotiation is a process, that there are no magic words that can suddenly change a suicidal or distressed person's mindset. However, he feels strongly that in this particular case, Elizabeth's words worked their magic. Communication is indeed an art form.

Chapter Thirteen

Words Can Hurt (Attempted Suicide)

Crisis negotiator Gilbert Wong

You wish to convey a caring message to a loved one with good intentions. However, the recipient misreads the message and its accompanying cues. The consequences of that misconception accumulate and explode with unimaginable intensity, with fatal results. Words can hurt! Words have the potential to scar a person for life and even drive her/him to contemplating suicide.

On a hot summer morning in 2012, an elderly woman in her late seventies was found sitting on the top of a small concrete platform mounted on the outer wall of a public housing building many floors above the ground in Kowloon. That structure is installed outside and beneath the residential units' windows. It was designed to hold air-conditioner units. Such a unit has a top cover and a base at the bottom. Apparently, the old woman had climbed through the window of her flat to reach that spot. It is not built for carrying a human's weight, and definitely it is not a place upon which to sit.

Gilbert Wong joined the PNC in 1999. He was called to the scene to try to defuse the crisis. He learned that the elderly woman had several children. They had floated with their mother the idea of moving her to an elderly home, where she would receive better care. Their mother was frail and weak and could hardly cook for herself. As yet, nothing was set in concrete.

The negotiator had no time to delve into the details of when and how the communication took place and what was said. He was racing against time. The old woman was in imminent danger of accidentally falling as a result of fatigue.

Gilbert positioned himself by the window inside the flat and as near to the lady as possible. The woman had short grey hair and was of slim build. Her eyebrows were knitted together in an expression of utter misery. Tears streamed down her cheeks. Her feet were dangling. She looked forlorn and distraught.

'Hello, Po Po[2]! I am Wong. How are you? I am here to help and listen to you. Have you had something to eat?'

The woman mumbled something occasionally, but she did not speak coherently. From the bits and pieces that the negotiator gathered from her talk, he learned what had driven her to such desperation. The elderly woman was heartbroken by the fact that her children intended to move her to a home for the elderly. She had convinced herself they had undoubtedly conspired to abandon her there to die of loneliness and despair. She had worked very hard in her youth to bring up the children, yet they were abandoning her (or so she thought). She would rather die than be abandoned in such a home.

---

[2] Po Po is a direct translation from the Chinese characters. It literally means grandmama. In the Chinese culture, one can address an old lady as Po Po out of respect even though she is not related.

In the meantime, the firemen had begun to abseil slowly down along the outer wall until they were just one floor above the lady's flat. They were preparing to assist in effecting the rescue when the time was fortuitous. A rescue cushion was also laid on the ground.

'I'd rather die now. I'd rather die now,' the woman wailed softly. At one point, she tensed up her body, tightened her jaw, and tried to rise from her sitting position.

'Don't move! Don't move! Po Po, stay where you are! I am concerned for your safety. Sit down. Sit back down!' Gilbert commanded the old lady in a voice that was authoritative yet empathetic. He did not show any trace of apprehension.

'Po Po, tell me about your younger days,' the negotiator urged. He paused and quietly observed the elderly lady as she searched through her memory.

She began, 'I was a beautiful girl when I was young. Many men wished to date me.'

'Oh, I see. Many men wished to date you. You are a beautiful lady. I would love to hear more. What happened then?' Gilbert continued to engage her in active listening. She talked about the happy times in her younger years. Her sad expression gradually softened. There was a visible change in her mood. The negotiator focused on that breakthrough. He showered her with admiration and asked a female colleague to join in their conversation.

Gilbert did not allow time for the woman to lapse back into morbidity or cultivate much pause to facilitate thinking time for the woman. There was relief when she said, 'I don't wish to die anymore.'

'Po Po, you have made an excellent decision. You remain where you are. There is no need for you to do anything. The firemen will come down from the upper floor to secure you and help you go back into your home. That's right. You are doing well.' Gilbert talked the old lady through what she had to do. All the time, he held her arm gently to reassure her. The episode lasted for slightly over thirty minutes, but it felt like an eternity. Everyone felt a great sense of relief when she was brought to safety.

Well, it was not over yet. Gilbert faced another challenging situation. Once inside the flat, the old lady sat down and fumbled with her purse. She carefully took out a stack of money and arranged it in order of denomination size. She counted and recounted it. Before anyone could figure out what the woman was trying to do, she called Gilbert to her side.

'Sir, thank you for being my good listener. You are a good man. Here, take this.' She then put several thousand dollars into Gilbert's hands.

'Po Po, I can't take the money. Please take it back.'

'No, no, no. You take it. Take it! You have helped me so much. I must reward you! It is not just for you. The firemen and all the police officers have helped me. Distribute the money evenly amongst yourselves.'

'Po Po, listen to me. It is illegal for us to take your money. You cannot do that. I really can't accept your money.'

This exchange continued, but Po Po would not be deterred. Gilbert then requested that the police incident commander come forward. 'Po Po, do you see this lady in uniform? She is a very senior police officer. Giving money to us for doing you service is illegal. We are delighted that you are safe. This lady will arrest me for bribery if I take your money!'

'Po Po, what he says is true. He's been so good to you and has listened with a good heart to your story. You don't want him to go to prison because of you, do you?' The incident commander put on a serious face as she said this. However, there was an undertone of kindness in her voice. She did not want to distress the old lady.

'You are a good person, you are,' the old lady said again and again as she put the money back into her purse.

At that point, Gilbert said, 'Po Po, there is something you can do for me. Take this little booklet and read it.' He handed her a guidebook on how to handle deliberate self-harm.

She opened it and said, 'The words are very small.'

A picture of a front and back cover of a guidebook on how to handle deliberate self-harm. Courtesy of the Hong Kong Jockey Club Centre for Suicide Research and Prevention, University of Hong Kong.

'Ask your children to read the contents to you. Tell them to read the booklet too. See these questions here: Why do people do things to harm themselves? If ever you wish to harm yourself, what should you do? There are quite a few useful tips here.' Gilbert opened the book to page eleven and continued. 'Po Po, do you see this page in green? On this page is a Positive Action Card. You can remove the card easily. Just pull the card out along the dotted line. I would like you to think of four things that you could do to lift your spirits whenever you feel unhappy. Write the four things down here. For example, you can sit down and take deep breaths, call your children, talk to them, and explain why you are so unhappy. You can sit down with your children and work out other suggestions, which you can use. Also, write down the name and telephone number of the person you will call if ever you feel lonely or unhappy. Your children love you very much and care a lot about you.'

'Sir, thank you for being my good listener. Thank you, thank you.' The old woman wrapped her palms around Gilbert's hands and nodded in gratitude.

A picture of the front side of two Positive Action Cards. The Chinese characters mean 'What to do in an emergency'. There are two cards inside each booklet. One is a sample card, and the other one is left blank for a person to fill in her/his own suggestions. The two cards can be easily detached. Courtesy of The Hong Kong Jockey Club Centre for Suicide Research and Prevention, University of Hong Kong.

緊急應對卡（Positive Action Card）

當我們有自毀傾向時，我們可以用以下的緊急應對卡，幫助我們冷靜下來。以下步驟只作參考，重點是要選擇合適自己的冷靜方法。

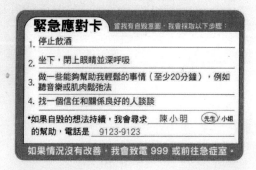

A picture of the back side of two Positive Action Cards.
Courtesy of the Hong Kong Jockey Club Centre for Suicide
Research and Prevention, University of Hong Kong.

The message in Chinese on the upper card, which is a sample, is translated as:

When we have thoughts of doing self-harm, we can refer to the advice written on this positive action card to help us calm down. The suggestions mentioned here are for reference. It is important to adopt the suggestions that are suitable to me.

When I have thoughts of doing self-harm, I shall take the following action to help me calm down:

1. Stop taking alcohol;

2. Sit down, close my eyes, and take deep breaths;

3. Do something that may help me to relax. For example, listening to relaxing music or doing some relaxing exercise for at least twenty minutes;

4. Talk to someone that I feel comfortable talking with.

*If I still have thoughts of self-harm, I shall seek help from Chan Siu-Ming, telephone no. 91239123.

If my situation has not improved, I shall dial 999 for help or proceed to a hospital's emergency room.

The message in Chinese on the lower card is translated as:

When I have thoughts of doing self-harm, I shall try out the following suggestions to help me calm down:

1. (blank)

2. (blank)

3. (blank)

4. (blank)

*If I still have thoughts of self-harm, I shall seek help from (blank), telephone no. (blank). If my situation has not improved, I shall dial 999 for help or proceed to a hospital's emergency room.

Gilbert's reflection

The elderly lady was entrapped in her own stubborn and probably unwarranted belief that her children had abandoned her. In such a depressed state, she could not accept Gilbert's assertion that this was not the case. Using active listening skills, he patiently listened to her while trying to find a hook that might change her mindset. He and all the others present were very worried that she might fall accidentally. He was racing against time.

After the lady was brought to safety, he took time talking to her. He gave her a booklet, *Deliberate Self-Harm, a Guide for You, Your families, Friends*, published in October 2013 jointly by the Hong Kong University and the Hong Kong Jockey Club Centre for Suicide Research and Prevention.

The booklet is in Chinese. The first half is directed towards people who are intent on self-harm. It explains in simple terms what is deliberate self-harm and encourages a person in distress to seek help and to communicate the self-harm intent to someone whom he/she trusts. The second half is directed towards friends and families of a person who feels distressed and is in need of assistance. The booklet provides some tips on dos and don'ts.

Communication

What is the consequence of miscommunication? The children had wished their frail mother to receive better care. They had given consideration to placing her in a home for elderly people. They explained their reasoning to their mother and suggested it to her. However, the elderly lady had her own notion of what that meant to her and resorted to contemplation of an extreme act of self-harm. It is not uncommon that a well-meaning intention is misconstrued by the person who is the recipient of that intention.

The old lady might already have formed a bad impression of what life in an elderly home would be like. She might have selectively listened to part of the children's conversation and then become ensnared by her fear of being left alone to perish in such a home. The children might well have been unaware of their mother's trepidation about moving to an elderly home.

Gilbert patiently listened to the elderly lady. Upon touching a positive subject, he encouraged her to indulge in reminiscences about her youth. That was the crucial turning point in their communication. Behavioural change kicked in, and the elderly lady aborted her suicidal attempt.

To this date, it is standard practice for the police negotiators to provide this booklet to suicidal persons after they have been saved. The booklet provides an additional channel for reaching out to people in distress and for people who notice a family or friend in need of emotional support to seek help.

Chapter Fourteen

We All Spoke at the Same Time; It Was the Right Time (Barricade)

Crisis negotiators Sindy Chan and Gilbert Wong

It was well after ten at night on a hot summer's day in 2012 when police received an urgent 999 call for help from a woman whose son was being held captive by her boyfriend.

A total of nine police negotiators turned out and worked together in this barricade incident. They took turns, in groups of three to four, to conduct the negotiation. Each session lasted approximately one and a half hours. The negotiation continued for over seven hours, until after six the following morning. The team did something unconventional—and it worked. Amongst them, Sindy Chan and Gilbert Wong shared their experience.

'Mom, help me! He's going to kill me!' A mother in her late thirties watched in helpless horror as her boyfriend pulled her eight-year-old son up the narrow stairs and into a foot massage parlour. He then locked the premises from the inside.

The members of the tactical team, the emergency unit of Kowloon West Region, were already on standby in the vicinity, in full tactical gear. A police officer from the tactical team quietly walked up to the entrance door and peeped inside through a glass pane on the door.

'Floor area slightly over a hundred square feet. At twelve o'clock position: three massage chairs. At two o'clock position: two windows, all covered up with paper and a ventilation fan on the top. Doorknob structure ...' The police officer reported the setting inside the premises to his team. The woman also told the police that there was a latch that locked the door from the inside. With this information, the tactical team constructed a contingency plan should they have to break into the premises on the orders of the police incident commander.

While waiting for the Police Negotiation Cadre (PNC) to arrive, the uniformed police officers had cordoned off the building which housed the massage parlour. They had gathered background information from the mother and witnesses. The woman was a widow. She ran a foot massage parlour all on her own. It was a small-scale business; she was the only masseuse. Her eight year-old son would join her at the parlour in the afternoon.

A few months ago, a man in his late forties patronised the massage parlour and became a regular customer. The woman and the man developed an intimate relationship. However, the woman soon found out that the man was an inveterate gambler and was heavily in debt.

Just after ten in the evening that night, the man turned up at the massage parlour. He looked flushed and asked his girlfriend to lend him several thousand dollars. She refused to do so. He hit her and grabbed a knife, threatening to kill her and her son. He chased them down the stairs onto the street. They screamed for help. In a fury, the man grabbed the boy in a headlock, dragged him up the stairs, and barricaded themselves in the foot massage parlour. The premises was located on the mezzanine floor of a tenement building. It was accessible only by a narrow staircase. The building had no lift.

When the PNC team arrived soon after, the man had drawn a curtain to cover the glass pane on the door. Through a small gap between the curtain and the glass pane, the negotiator saw that the man was holding a cutter against the neck of the boy.

For the first hour or so, the man was very defensive and talked angrily. Every sentence he uttered was full of expletives. 'All I wanted was several thousand dollars. If she had given it to me, none of this would have happened!' The man continued his rant and blamed his girlfriend and the neighbours for what was transpiring. The negotiator engaged the man in active listening, trying to calm his emotions.

Several hours went by. Through a small corner of the window pane that was not covered by the curtain, the negotiator saw that the man had loosened his grip on the boy. Only when the boy walked near the door once or twice could he be seen.

'How is the boy? Is he OK?' one negotiator asked the man.

'Uh, he is sleeping in a corner,' the man replied after a while, and then he called to the boy in a gentle tone. 'Eh, boy, are you alright?' The man told the negotiator that he was fine. 'Look. I didn't do anything to the kid. I didn't harm him.'

The man's reply gave the negotiators an invaluable clue. He did not seem to be hostile towards the boy. Despite this fact, the man stood his ground and refused to open the door.

More than five hours had passed. The police incident commander was considering the option of breaking down the door by force. The team leader of the PNC discussed the situation with the incident commander. Eventually, the incident commander decided that the police negotiators would continue talking to the man.

'Hey, man, the most senior police officer at the scene is thinking of instructing his men to break the door down. Their equipment is very effective. It would take no time for them to break down the lock, enter, and arrest you. Do you know why they haven't yet done this? It is because my team members and I have been reporting the progress we have made to him. We observe that you are not a violent person. You have not hurt the boy. We are telling the incident commander that we are confident that we can resolve the incident peacefully,' one negotiator said.

'Don't let them come in. Don't let them come near me. Will they shoot me? Are they going to shoot me?' the man responded nervously. He was in a state of alarm. His eyes darted from the door to the windows and then to the ventilation fan.

'Guy, listen to me. Calm down. Listen to me. This is Hong Kong. Police officers in Hong Kong will not shoot you unless you are threatening to do grave harm to the boy or some other person. Are you going to do that?' one negotiator asked the man. The man shook his head and vowed that he did not intend to hurt anybody.

'I am glad to hear that. What I understand is this. You lost your temper because your girlfriend refused to lend you any money. You hit her, threatened her with a knife, and detained the boy. You broke the law, but you are not a notorious criminal. You have not committed any grave crime, like murder or arson. You have not harmed the boy. The uniformed police officers could have stormed the flat a long time ago. Why didn't they do that? Do you know why they didn't? They trust us. They have faith in the police negotiators. We have been talking to you for so many hours; we act as a bridge between you and those police officers.'

Two negotiators took turns to convey this message to the man and let him consider his position. The man's reply indicated that he was coming to his senses.

The rest of the PNC team members spoke together, one following another. They felt it was the right moment to reinforce the positive messages, which they were trying to impress upon the man. Two voices increased to four, then to six. Eventually, all of them chorus-like, spoke to the man.

'You have done the right thing. You did not harm the boy.'

'Yeah, you have done the right thing. You are not a bad person at heart.'

'We can resolve this peacefully.'

'When you are ready, open the door and hand over the boy to us. No one will harm you. But you have to understand the policeman will arrest you. You did commit a crime.'

'You just need to take one more step. You open this door now, and this episode will be over. One step more.'

'Yeah, just one more step, man. You can do it.' The whole team of negotiators kept talking in that manner.

In the midst of those encouraging words, the man opened the door and pushed the boy in front of him as he walked out. An officer of the tactical team came forward to rescue the boy. Another officer stepped forward to handcuff the man and lead him down the stairs to the police vehicle.

Gilbert and Sindy's reflection

The man was prone to outbursts of temper. He remained stubborn and defensive for a very long period. In time, the PNC team assessed that the man had found himself in a dire situation and did not know how to extract himself from it. They let him vent his anger, and over time he became more rational and less threatening.

The PNC team then did something unusual in the negotiation process. It is a general rule or understanding that one negotiator talks to a subject person at a time. If more than one negotiator talks, they do it in turn and explain to the subject person the reason for the change of speaker.

This scenario presented an uncommon opportunity that all the negotiators present felt it was the right moment and appropriate thing to do: to speak to the man as a team, all at the same time. Their success was more than fortuitous. It was the result of a professional, close-knit, team strategy. Rationally and intuitively, they knew that this was the best course of action to resolve the situation that had manifested itself.

Communication

This case is an apt demonstration of intelligence-led negotiation and communication. The uniformed police officers collected useful information, which they relayed to the PNC team. The PNC reported regularly to the police incident commander so he could base his decision-making on what was happening in real time.

As the hours dragged on, no one knew when the crisis would end. The negotiators persevered, never losing their drive to resolve the crisis. Eventually, they were able to persuade the man to surrender and release the boy unharmed. This episode demonstrated the power of communication.

A painting, 'Sunrise', by Karma Castilho.

She invites the viewer, whose life is hectic or troubled,
to surrender to the serenity of the scene.

Let your mind infiltrates this scene. The hills slope gently, blending
harmoniously with the level stretch of land below. The sun's rays
quietly but gloriously bring light to the day; the waves caress
the shore ever so softly. Your mind's eye contemplates the sky
above. Earth's winged creatures glide effortlessly over the water.
Your thoughts and feelings merge, seduced and delighted by
this sense of calmness and stillness. You share the experience
with all those human beings who have stood in the same spot
and been filled with marvel and the sense of the eternal.

We invite our police negotiators to participate in this mystery
and joy of life with Karma. When you are tired and overworked,
take the time to pause and dwell upon this scene of affirmation
and renewal. Feel the warm sun kissing your cheek. Let it
nourish and reinvigorate you. Take your time. You deserve it
as the guardians of the sanctity of life. Move on when you
are ready. Move on to even greater deeds in your life.

Part E:

THE FOURTH C—
CONTROL OF EMOTION

Chapter Fifteen

Upside Down Logic (Barricade)

Crisis negotiator Calvin Cheung

For a man or woman addicted to drugs, life revolves around his/her ability to feed this insatiable appetite. No amount of love or motherly affection can deter that person from scoring his/her next heroin shot. The addict oftentimes refuses to accept responsibility for his/her addiction. Often that person seeks to place that blame at the feet of others, especially on those people who constitute his immediate family. In the case of the negotiator, he/she strives to be non-judgemental. To the negotiator, every life is valuable. Every life is worth saving. In this particular case, the negotiator persuades a heroin addict with a notorious criminal record to put down his chopper and surrender himself to the police.

Early in the evening, the police received a report that a man in his early fifties had barricaded himself inside his home in a public housing estate in the New Territories. He had injured his mother earlier on, was in possession of a knife, and was threatening to kill himself if the police attempted a forced entry into the flat. He had locked the iron gate and the wooden door.

The police requested that the Police Negotiation cadre (PNC) attend the scene to defuse the crisis. Calvin Cheung, who had joined the PNC in July 2006, assumed the role of negotiator in this case. He was a police constable at that time.

According to the mother, her son had no work. Each day, he demanded a hundred odd dollars from his mother to buy heroin. If she declined, he would shout abuse at her and even hit her. In the end, she always gave in. She did not make any report to the police. It had been like this for years.

Three days ago, the mother steadfastly refused to give money to her son to feed his drug habit. Without the drug, he experienced nausea, a runny nose, and sometimes pangs of delirium. On this particular day, he had rampaged through his mother's purse, desperate for money to satisfy his addiction. However, his mother had hidden the money elsewhere. In a rage, he grabbed a chopper from the kitchen and attacked her. His mother rushed out of the flat and screamed for help. Neighbours helped her make her escape and quickly reported the incident to the police.

The police had conducted a check on the man's background. He had an extensive criminal record and had been a heroin drug addict for many years.

When Calvin started talking to the man behind the doors, the man responded with hostility, and his words were full of expletives. 'Who's there? I have a chopper. Go away! You come in, and I'll kill myself!'

'Hey, man, I'm Cheung. I'm a police negotiator. Would you like to tell me what happened?'

'What do you care? Mind your own business. Tell all the policemen to f--- off!'

'I have come to offer you help and listen to you. What is the reason for locking yourself in the flat? Are you hurt? I can call an ambulance for you.'

'What ambulance? The ambulance took that damn woman to the hospital. I heard the siren.'

'The woman was taken to the hospital. Is she your mother? Would you like to tell me what happened?'

'Umm ...' the man grunted.

'Hey, you do not sound well. Can you open the wooden door so we can see each other while we talk? You can keep the iron gate locked. I won't force you to do anything.'

There was more grunting and groaning from the man. 'It is all her fault—she makes me lose my temper. I don't need a lot, just a hundred bug, but she has to play hard to get. I'm feeling horrible, but she does not care. Just keep telling me to give it up. That job she finds me. All bullshit!'

The man continued his rant. It was evident to everyone present that he was selfish and self-centred. He distorted the circumstances of his addiction and put all the blame on his mother. There was only one version of things—his version. He was without remorse for what he had done to his mother.

The police officers of the tactical team felt the man was a hardened criminal and had no sympathy for him. There was talk of impatience and storming into the flat so as to bring the matter to a close quickly. The negotiator gestured to the police officers to stay put and keep calm. He acknowledged the man's emotion and grievances towards his mother. He maintained a non-threatening tone. Even though the man could not see him, he maintained a neutral expression on his face. At one point, he requested a time-out, and another PNC team partner took over for a while. The negotiator needed to vent his frustration and anger, but without the man knowing it. When he returned, he continued to try to see what was transpiring from the man's point of view.

Hours passed. The man babbled and complained non-stop. In time, Calvin asked him, 'You have talked a lot about yourself. You are not happy with life. What do you want exactly?' The man made a specific request. After some thought, the negotiator said, 'OK, it can be done. You can have it.'

Next, Calvin spoke to the police officers in the hearing of the man, 'Step back, guys. More ... more, please. Leave a good amount of space in front of the door.' The negotiator did something and told the man that it was done.

Not long after, there was a noise. The man opened the wooden door. He made eye contact with the police officers. Nobody said anything. The man opened the iron gate, and the tactical team rushed forward to subdue and handcuff him. He did not put up any resistance. He did not bother to glance at whom he had been talking to for all that time. There was no mention of the promised deed.

Calvin's reflection

The man was suffering from the withdrawal symptoms of heroin addiction. He acted impulsively and irrationally. As the negotiation progressed, the man had reconnected with reality at some point, albeit partially. Caught in a stalemate for so many hours, he needed someone to tell him how to proceed. Thinking out of the box, the negotiator asked what the man wanted. The man made a request. Calvin considered that the request was not difficult to fulfil, and he acceded to it. When the man opened the two doors and came out, he paid no attention to the deed performed by the negotiator. In a way, the man needed a platform to surrender.

After careful consideration, the negotiator felt that it was best not to disclose what the request was. He assures the reader that the man did not make a request for a heroin shot.

Control of Emotion

The man was in a confrontational mood. Through his perseverance and patience, the negotiator managed to keep the man's
emotions in check, and he eventually persuaded him to end
the impasse.

In this scenario, the negotiator had to control the frustration of
the tactical team and his own judgemental feelings towards the
man's arrogance and sense of twisted logic.

Chapter Sixteen

'All for One, One for All' (Triple Attempted Suicide Pact)

Crisis negotiator Elizabeth Ma

Three teenage girls shared a few things in common. They did not understand most of the subjects taught in class. They were at the bottom in all their academic studies. They took pride in talking back to the teachers.

'All for one, one for all.' This famous quote from Alexandre Dumas's novel *The Three Musketeers* might well have applied to the three girls. Indeed, one might be tempted to call them by the names of principal characters from the novel, in order to preserve their anonymity. However, attempted suicide is too serious an event to consider this use of allusion. For the sake of clarity of understanding, we need to differentiate amongst the three girls. They are thus assigned the names of Iris, Peony, and Tulip.

The three musketeers made a pact that they would commit suicide together. A police negotiator attempted to avert such a tragic outcome.

The school year had just started. On a particular day, the police received a report that three teenage girls in school uniform were drinking beer on the top platform of a water tank on the roof-top of a commercial building in Kowloon. The building was over twenty storeys high. At one point, the girls threw pieces of paper off the building. Written on the papers were their grievances against the school authorities. The private secondary school which the girls attended was on the lower floors.

A picture of the rooftop of the building depicted in the scenario.
The concrete block circled in black was the water tank. The
photo was taken in 2018 during the writing of this book.

The building was situated on a major thoroughfare. The police had cordoned off a long stretch of the road. The fire services had laid out a rescue cushion on the ground, a precaution should the worst possible scenario manifest itself. Traffic virtually came to a standstill across the Kowloon Peninsula.

The girls threatened to jump if anyone attempted to go near them. The platform had no parapet. All that was required was a few steps to reach the edge.

A picture of the top platform of the water tank depicted
in the scenario. A black arrow indicates the water tank.
It was taken in 2018 during the writing of this book.

Elizabeth Ma was a member of the Police Negotiation Cadre (PNC) from 1989 to 2007 until her retirement. She was a senior inspector of police at the time of this particular incident.

That day was an important date for Elizabeth. She was preparing to participate in a photo-taking ceremony at the Hong Kong Baptist University. This was to recognise the fact that she had been awarded a bachelor's degree in arts (English). At her office in the police station, she looked at herself in the mirror for the last touch-up. She put on her high-heel shoes and was ready to leave.

There was a knock on her door. The duty officer of the police station informed her that an incident involving a triple suicide pact was ongoing nearby. Without second thought, Elizabeth raced to the scene in her cheongsam (a Chinese one-piece long gown) and high-heel shoes.

Before approaching the girls, the negotiator learned about the background of the three musketeers from the school authorities and the details written on the leaflets which they had thrown to the ground. They had completed nine years' compulsory free education in other local schools. They were the bottom performers. Their parents sent them to that private secondary school to finish forms four and five (grade ten and eleven). They could not care less what the teachers taught in class. On that day during class, they were angry because they felt that their teacher had disciplined them unfairly. They left the classroom abruptly, without the teacher's permission.

The negotiator needed one more piece of information. Who was the ringleader amongst the three?

She arrived at the rooftop. To establish eye contact with the trio, she had to climb a set of thin, metal ladders which led to the top of a water tank, where the girls had positioned themselves. She stationed herself midway on the ladder, where she could see the girls. She was just a few feet away from them.

vertical ladder

A picture of the ladder depicted in the scenario. Apparently, the three girls climbed up this ladder to reach the platform. The negotiator stationed herself midway on the ladder. The photo was taken in 2018 during the writing of this book.

There was no parapet surrounding the platform where the girls sat. Several empty beer bottles were lying around them; some were broken. Each of the girls had cut wounds on their left wrists. Spilt beer mixed with blood formed a puddle of reddish liquid on the ground.

The negotiator paced herself. She sought to communicate but not command. She acknowledged their unhappiness and empathised with them. She then remained silent, giving the girls time and space to think and reflect upon her words.

Elizabeth thought it was a good sign that Iris started talking first. The girls' teacher informed the negotiator that Iris, the chatterbox, was the ringleader. The other two gradually joined in the conversation. The negotiator listened patiently. It was not her role to pass judgement. They expressed grievances against the school authorities, the teachers, and their male classmates. They had no interest in studying. They had no skills. They could not see any point in finishing forms four and five.

There was talking ...
There was active listening ...
There was encouragement ...
There was silence ...
There was anger ...
There was sobbing ...
There was anguish ...
There was sisterly affection ...
There was hope ...

Elizabeth thought she was on the right track in focusing on the empowerment of Iris, the supposed ringleader. She focused on trying to convince Iris that she had a responsibility to ensure the well-being of her friends. Elizabeth drew Iris's attention to the pale-faced Tulip, whose facial and body language seemed to indicate the reality of the dire position which they had placed themselves in was beginning to dawn on her. Tulip was encouraged to accept help. In time, Tulip got up and was helped down the stairs.

As soon as Tulip left, Elizabeth noticed a change in the atmosphere. Iris and Peony fell into an awkward silence, and with their heads down, they looked at each other occasionally with hollow expressions. Elizabeth was taken aback when she received information from her PNC team that the school teacher had made a mistake. Tulip, the girl who had left, was the ringleader of the group.

Nevertheless, she continued to speak in a reassuring tone. She let the girls see that hope was within their grasps. Eventually, Iris moved. Not long afterwards, Peony got up too. However, Peony was still holding a broken beer bottle in one hand. Remaining poised as the girl approached, Elizabeth said, 'You don't need that anymore.' She calmly reached out to take the broken bottle out of Peony's hand and then helped her down the stairs.

The immediate problem was to shield the three girls from the eager reporters waiting downstairs. Elizabeth promised the reporters that she would provide a full account of the incident in exchange for an uninterrupted pathway from the building to the ambulance. Both sides kept their promises.

The drama lasted for about one and a half hour. After the girls were escorted away, traffic and people's lives gradually returned to normal.

Elizabeth's reflection

Elizabeth learnt from case sharing sessions in crisis negotiation that a ringleader of a group in a crisis controls essential dynamics. The leader may be the instigator of a radical act; he/she is the protector of a group's well-being. The members look up to their leader for reassurance and direction. Elizabeth thus worked out a plan to empower the ringleader of her responsibility and guide her to see to the needs of her group members. She perceived that the girls would be more inclined to listen to their team leader's words than her.

As soon as the true ringleader of the triple suicide pact group was mistakenly taken off, Elizabeth immediately sensed there was something amiss in the relationship between the other two girls. They lost support and protection when their leader was gone. Fortunately, Elizabeth reacted quickly. As a result of the trust that Elizabeth engendered in the girls, they too came down from the rooftop.

The senior management and many colleagues in the police force complimented Elizabeth on her calmness and the high degree of expertise, which she utilised in bringing the crisis to a successful resolution.

After that, many secondary schools in Hong Kong invited her to give talks to students. 'No matter how old you are, what stage of life you are in, you and I will come across difficulties. When you feel lonely or sad and see no way out, be kind to yourself. You are not alone. Talk to someone you trust.' This is Elizabeth's recurring message in her talks.

Control of Emotion

Elizabeth gained the trust and friendship of the girls through active listening and not being judgemental or lecturing them. After they had an avenue to express their anger and frustration, the girls calmed down. Elizabeth's plan was to convince the leader that she had a moral responsibility to ensure the safety and well-being of her friends. In time, the girls were guided to feel hope and a way in which they could extricate themselves from a perilous situation.

The negotiator also satisfied the needs of the news reporters. She promised to give them a full account of the incident. The girls were thus protected from further emotional damage. In the same professional way, she provided a full account of the incident to senior officers.

Authors' note

Elizabeth was unable to provide concrete details of what she and the girls talked about. The lapse of time between when the incident occurred and being invited to provide an account of the episode left her with no specific recollection of the conversation which had transpired. Thus, in order to depict that period, when the girls' emotions had swirled and swung like a roller coaster, Connie summarised that period of communication using short, dynamic sentences, such as, 'There was talking; there was listening; there was encouragement.'

Chapter Seventeen

A Burglar Needs a Platform to Surrender (Barricade)

Crisis negotiator Gilbert Wong

On a hot summer afternoon, a man had burgled several flats in a high-rise residential building. The outer wall of the building was under renovation. For the work to be carried out, bamboo scaffolding was erected from the ground to the top floor. The man had climbed up the scaffolding and entered the flats through unsecured windows. His act was discovered, and somebody dialled 999. The police soon arrived and cordoned off the building. He refused to take heed of police warnings to surrender.

A picture of bamboo scaffoldings in Hong Kong

A close-up picture of bamboo scaffolding in Hong Kong. The scaffolding is covered with a layer of mesh to prevent flying debris from falling to the pavement. They are similar to the type mentioned in this scenario.

'You rotten policemen downstairs. I am not coming down! I will jump if anyone dares to come near me!' the man shouted repeatedly. His speech was laced with expletives. He was on the scaffolding at the fifteenth storey. The Police Negotiation Cadre (PNC) was called in to handle the crisis.

Gilbert Wong joined the PNC in 1999. He and two team members responded to the scene. On the way, the PNC team obtained background information about the man. He had committed burglary before. Gilbert took up the role of negotiator. He was a senior inspector of police at the time of handling this incident.

A uniformed police officer was talking with the man. With the permission of a tenant, the police officer had stationed himself inside a flat's bedroom on the same floor as the man. The negotiator considered it best to assume the same spot and took over from the uniformed police officer.

Evening came to pass. While looking out through an opened window on the same floor, only two arms' length away, the negotiator saw the man sitting and occasionally standing on the bamboo rod of the scaffolding structure. The window frame was their only barrier.

'Hey, man. I am Wong. I have come here to talk to you and to assist you,' the negotiator opened the dialogue. Should he choose to look, the man could see the negotiator inside the lit room. Outside the building, the scaffolding was completely covered with mesh. The man was of short stature and thin build. Because the light was dim, the negotiator could not interpret the man's mood through his facial expression.

For the first hour or so, the man maintained a tirade of vulgar talk laced with expletives. He talked loudly and rapidly. His anger was obvious. However, so too was his anguish and fear. Sitting or standing on the bamboo rod was proving to be a difficult task. From time to time, due to tiredness, he had to change hands holding on to the rod. The surface beneath him was becoming slippery due to the fact that he was sweating profusely.

The negotiator listened patiently. He nodded to acknowledge the man's remarks. He remained non-judgemental. The man requested a cigarette and some water. This request was facilitated by the PNC team.

Not long after, the man needed to answer a call of nature. However, he refused the negotiator's offer to use the toilet inside the flat. Eventually, the negotiator passed a message through the pipeline to the police incident commander.

'Officers on the ground floor, stay clear of the scaffolding. The man is going to pee from the fifteenth floor!' the police incident commander said through the police beat radio.

There was an awkward silence, as the man relieved himself. A while later, he grunted, signalling that he had finished. In time, the man asked three questions and made one request. He respectfully addressed the negotiator as 'sir'.

'Don't arrest me. Can you promise?'

'Don't prosecute me. Can you promise?'

'Can you promise that you won't bash me if I turn myself in?'

'Contact my wife and ask her to come here. I've got something to say to her.'

In actual fact, the man did not utter them in a precise order. He mentioned them repeatedly and randomly throughout their dialogue. The man knew he was in no position to bargain. However, in order to let reality sink in, the negotiator had to skilfully manipulate the situation. As they talked, the pace of the man's speech gradually slowed down. The negotiator sensed that the man was less hostile. It was time to respond to those questions.

The first question was, 'Don't arrest me. Can you promise?' The negotiator spoke gently and sincerely. 'Do you really think that the police officers down below and I have a choice to let you go?' The negotiator put special emphasis when he spoke the word 'really'. A momentary silence ensued. In that stretch of time, reality dawned on the man, to such an extent that he chose to not persist with the question.

The second question was, 'Don't prosecute me. Can you promise?' The negotiator informed the man that the police's job is to apprehend a culprit, gather evidence, and build a case for the prosecution. The prerogative of prosecution rests with the department of justice. The police would gather all the facts of the case. He emphasised that the police would mention whether or not the defendant cooperated with the police investigation. It was not a direct reply of yes or no. The negotiator deliberately highlighted what mattered to the man. The prospect of cooperation appeared to strike a chord within the man. He became more attentive and was receptive to the negotiator's advice. All the while, the negotiator's tone was soothing and not aggressive.

The third question was, 'Could you promise you won't bash me if I turn myself in?' If the man raised such a question during a counselling session, it would be a good opportunity to delve into the man's history, especially his relationships with the police. This was not the time or place for such an investigation and analysis. Therefore, the negotiator decided not to enquire about the man's motivation in asking that question. The fact that the man asked such question was a very good indicator of his state of mind. He was probably contemplating turning himself in.

The negotiator phrased his reply in the form of a question. 'We have been talking like this for so long. Do you really think I would bash you when you walk in here?' Even though he could not see the man's face, the negotiator sensed that the man accepted the fact that he would not be set upon by the police. No further conversation on this matter transpired. However, the negotiator could sense the man's unblinking glare as these words registered in his mind.

The final request was, 'Contact my wife to come here. I've got something to say to her.' The PNC team had contacted his wife, but she declined to come to the scene. In any case, the man was beginning to listen to reason. The negotiator would handle this request later, when the crisis was resolved.

The negotiator went on to tell the man about the procedures that would follow, as if the man had agreed to come inside the flat. In the end, almost five hours into their talk, the man quietly climbed back into the flat through the opened window, at which time he surrendered. The negotiator told the man he was doing the right thing and then stepped back to make way for the uniformed police officers to perform their duties. The man was handcuffed, arrested, and eventually charged for having committed burglary.

Gilbert's reflection

The burglar was caught red-handed in his criminal act. Arresting him was only a matter of time, and he had no bargaining power. However, he behaved irrationally and asked challenging questions. Gilbert had to think quickly. He had to work out how to respond to the man's questions honestly, without alarming him and arousing his ire.

The negotiator listened patiently and made the man aware that someone was willing to listen to him. In doing so, a certain level of trust was gradually established between them. He monitored the man's emotions carefully and found the right time to address the questions.

It is not uncommon that the parties engaged in dialogue need to take a water or toilet break. In the case of the negotiator, he/she will inform the other party and be excused for that purpose while another team member will stand in his/her place. In this particular case, the negotiator did not take any break.

Conversely, a negotiator may offer a drink to the subject person or enquire if the person needs a toilet break. Sometimes when a negotiation drags on for a long time, thoughtful gestures like these can change an atmosphere of stalemate and lift the mood of the subject. If the subject initiates such requests, the negotiator can suggest to the person to move from her/his spot to have a drink or go to the toilet. For instance, 'You must be thirsty. Why don't you come and join me for a glass of ice-cold Coke? It will be so refreshing.' Or, 'Sure, I'll give you a hand. Come this way. The toilet is right over there.' The negotiator does not expressly tell the subject person to surrender. In a subtle way, it provides that person with a practical reason to abort the intended act of self-harm. Sometimes it works, and sometimes it doesn't.

Control of Emotion

The burglar behaved aggressively at the beginning. He had nowhere to escape, and surrendering was his only realistic choice. However, he decided to make the situation more difficult for the police. The negotiator took time listening to him and allowed him to vent his anger. In time, the man's anger began to dissipate. However, he posed questions of an awkward nature. By closely monitoring the man's emotions, the negotiator addressed the questions without arousing alarm or ire in the man. In the end, the negotiator provided a platform for the man to surrender peacefully and with his dignity relatively intact.

Chapter Eighteen

Coping with Pressure (Barricade)

Crisis negotiator Rachel Hui

When police officers retire, they need to adjust to a normal lifestyle. They have an abundance of time on their hands. A retired police officer found himself caught up in a frustrating interpersonal relationship with his family members.

On a morning in 2011, the police received a report that a man had quarrelled with his wife and was preventing her and their children from leaving their home in the New Territories.

The man refused to open the iron gate to the attending uniformed police officers. The police requested that the Police Negotiation Cadre (PNC) attend the scene. Rachel Hui joined the PNC in 2011. She was an inspector of police and had just completed her crisis negotiation training at the time of handling this incident.

She and her PNC team arrived outside the flat. The wooden door was open, but the iron gate was closed. She was able to see the man, who was sitting on the sofa in the living room. It did not take her long to discern that the man appeared to be quite knowledgeable about police procedures and police jargon. The negotiator engaged in active listening and acknowledged his grievances without passing judgement.

While looking through the iron gate, she saw a few framed documents hanging on the wall. They appeared to be written commendations issued by the Hong Kong police. She prompted the man to tell her what they were.

The man readily admitted he was a retired police officer. He had put all the important commendations awarded to him into glass frames and hung them on the wall. The negotiator showed respect and deference as the man described how those cases were resolved under his leadership. They reminisced on his good old days in the police force. In time, the man calmed down and softened his manner. He opened the iron gate voluntarily and invited the negotiator and her PNC team into the living room. The negotiator addressed him as 'senior brother'. She expressed great admiration for his professionalism and excellent detective work, which had earned him so many commendations.

When the man's wife and children realised that there was no longer any tension in the living room, they resumed their activities and did not feel alarmed anymore.

With some awkwardness, the man confessed a longstanding, strained relationship with his wife and children. 'When I used to work in the police station, my men were so respectful towards me. If I gave an order, it was an order, and things got done. Here, my wife complains that I order her around, but I'm only telling her to put things in order, that's all. The kids hardly listen to me. I drink sometimes; I have nothing to do. I feel so useless in this home. I am a nobody here. I can't stand it anymore. Today, I told them that we must all sit down. No one should leave until we talk things over. What was the fuss about dialling 999? I didn't do anything wrong, that's for sure. I don't wish to cause you trouble. I understand it's your job to resolve the situation.' It was not easy for him to bare his feelings.

In the end, he became friendly towards the negotiator. The incident ended peacefully. The negotiator suggested that counselling services as a possible option to cope with the family's tension.

Rachel's reflection

Police officers work forty-eight hours per week. Officers working in the crime detection department typically work very long hours. Most of the incidents they handle arise from other people's unhappy experiences—for instance, domestic dispute, suicide, and a vast array of criminal activities. They have to think and act quickly. They have to present a professional image to earn people's trust. Amongst colleagues, they have to appear to be competent and resourceful. They work under enormous pressure most of the time.

When it comes to personal problems, female police officers may confide in friends and colleagues. It is very often not easy for some male police officers to acknowledge that they are facing personal issues. Traditionally, it is not manly to expose one's vulnerabilities.

Adjustment to a retired life is not an easy path for some police officers. The man in this scenario had to leave behind his persona as a policeman and integrate into ordinary life. Having more time on his hand to spend with the family might also meant greater chances of conflict. Before old disagreements could be resolved, new ones would manifest themselves. Although he had calmed down after talking to the negotiator, the man would need to engage in some self-reflection on how to adjust to retired life and maintain a healthy relationship with his family.

Control of Emotion

With her keen powers of observation, the negotiator was soon able to ascertain that the man was, indeed, a former policeman. She expressed her admiration for his achievements as a police officer and showed great respect towards him. The man acknowledged that the negotiator understood and respected his role as a fellow police officer. They could communicate on the same wavelength. Negativity and agitation quickly gave way to cooperation and camaraderie. Agitated emotion transformed into a cooperative attitude.

However, the man's problems with his family were not resolved. He would need to address the cause of his outburst of emotions and find ways to cultivate a better relationship with his family.

Chapter Nineteen

Father and Son (Attempted Suicide)

Crisis negotiator Dr Gregory M. Vecchi, a retired FBI special agent

Dr Gregory Vecchi shared this story about a case that he handled in the United States. He was then a special agent in crisis negotiation with the FBI.

One day, Greg was called upon to assist another federal agency in the United States. A man had barricaded himself inside his house and was going to kill himself with his gun. Greg got on the phone and talked to the man.

'Hi, I'm Greg from the FBI. Are you OK?' Greg opened a dialogue by first introducing himself. Under the law in the United States he had to identify himself as a police officer. The man's reply was heavy with sadness, but he did not reject the negotiator's approach. From experience, some people might not like the police. To moderate the approach, Greg usually said that he was from the FBI. Most people were comfortable with such an introduction.

The negotiator learned that the man used to work in a prestigious company as an engineer, with a very specialised skill set. The job was his whole world. He brought home a sizeable pay cheque and lived an upper-middle-class lifestyle. Recently, he was laid off and could not find a job. In trying to maintain the same level of living standard for his family, he soon exhausted his savings. Unpaid bills began to mount up. He felt his loss of income was having an adverse effect on what he wanted to provide for his two boys. His despair progressed to the point that he could no longer cope with the pressure. Everything he had tried could not fix his mounting problems. If he killed himself, his family would receive a death benefit from his life insurance premium. Then, at least his boys would be taken care of. The man was in that mental state when the negotiator talked with him over the phone.

They had some initial conversation. 'Tell me about your family,' Greg said, and then he paused.

The pause almost obliged the man to respond.

'I've got two great boys,' the man replied.

'Wow, you really love your sons.'

'Yeah, of course I love my sons.'

'Tell me more about what you do with them,' Greg said before pausing once more.

'My boys love the outdoor life. I take them hiking, fishing, and hunting. I still recall the shrieks and joy on his face when my younger son caught his first fish. He was five then. He was so determined to handle the live bait all by himself. He hooked a live worm on the hook. I only had to show him once. And the two boys managed to communicate only by hand gestures for a whole hour, because they didn't wish to scare away the fish. This was just as I told them. The whole atmosphere was hilarious. I couldn't figure out what they were communicating about, but they seemed to understand each other. Ah, we had such great times together. On one occasion, my elder son and I were in a lift full of elderly ladies. When the lift reached the ground floor, my son held the lift for all the ladies to get out first and then gestured for me to exit. I looked at him wide-eyed. He said, "Dad, I follow your example. Ladies first," and he grinned at me. I was so proud of my son.'

'You are a good provider and a great dad,' Greg responded.

'I try to be. I make it a point to bring them out to the countryside every weekend. No matter what happens, my boys always come first. But I can't do it anymore. I can't afford the high tuition fees and the outdoor expenses. The payout from my life insurance premium should be sufficient to pay for their college fees. At least I could guarantee that,' the man said with a heavy sigh, and he went silent.

Greg listened. He had not said anything other than to reflect and stay in the man's frame of reference. In that process, the man felt better and was less agitated. Greg then provided a statement and remained quiet. It was a not a question, not a judgement. 'You know what, John? If you killed yourself today, your sons are going to lose their best friend.'

Shortly, Greg could hear heavy breathing, and the man started crying. The negotiator gave him space and time.

'You are right.' The man uttered these three words and then broke down into heavy sobs. Greg knew that now the man was able to think rationally.

'Hey, look, why don't you come out and let's talk about it? Let's get this resolved. I've got resources. I've got some ideas. I'm happy to talk to you about it. It doesn't have to be this way.'

The man had identified Greg as his social support and was ready to listen to coping strategies. Greg then provided the resources to deescalate the situation and gave him hope.

'Let's make this happen, John. Here's what's going to happen. There are some guys out there. They are in uniform, and they've got guns and equipment. I'll tell them that you are going to come out. They are not going to hurt you. When you come out, you will be met by these officers. You've got a gun with you?' The man's reply was affirmative. 'I want you to put your gun down and leave any sharp items behind in the house. After you put the gun down and leave the sharp items in the house, open the door, raise your hand, and show us your palms. The uniformed guys will approach you. They are not going to hurt you. For your safety and everyone else's safety, they will do a quick search on you and handcuff you. That's a requirement. They do that for safety reasons. They will take you down to the station, and they are going to talk to you. They are going to help you. You can do it. I'll guide you through.' The man followed Greg's guidance and surrendered.

Greg's reflection

When the man was in a state of crisis, he reacted emotionally and lost the ability to reason. At that stage, Greg would not try to reason with the man. Instead, he engaged in empathetic, active listening to build rapport and trust. When the man mentioned that he had two great boys, Greg immediately followed up. The man wanted to be the best role model for his sons. He taught them different skill sets, to be a good provider like him, and to respect women.

Greg stayed in his frame of reference and acknowledged his feelings. Through active listening, the negotiator recognised that his sons meant everything to the man. His mood gradually lightened. Then, Greg provided a statement that his sons would lose their best friend if the man killed himself. That was a very powerful, awakening dynamic for the man. The statement touched him profoundly; he was now ready to think rationally. A behavioural change had taken place. Greg then guided the man, step by step, on how to surrender. By telling the man 'when you come out' but not 'if you come out', Greg reinforced the sense of certainty in the man's thinking. This case is an excellent example of the application of his Behavioral Influence Stairway Model (BISM) in suicidal crisis situations (Vecchi et al. 2019, 230–39).

BEHAVIORAL INFLUENCE STAIRWAY MODEL

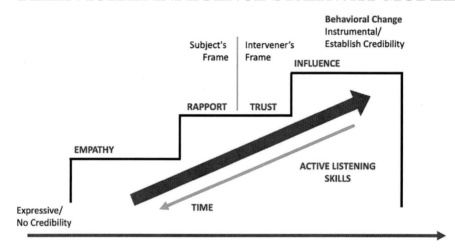

A diagram of the Behavioral Influence Stairway Model (BISM), courtesy of Dr Gregory M Vecchi. The original version of the BISM was created by Mr Gary Nosener, former chief of the FBI's Crisis Negotiation Unit, Critical Incident Response Group and was subsequently documented by Dr Vecchi.

Control of Emotion

Step by step, Greg guided the man to the point where he wanted to talk about his two great boys. As the man talked about his boys and what he did with them to develop their characters, his mood lifted, and his pride in his boys became very evident.

When Greg provided a statement to the man that his sons would lose their best friend if he killed himself, the man was profoundly moved. In the man's heart of hearts, he knew that this was true. The statement was a powerful awakening. He was ready to listen and respond to talk of coping strategies.

Part F:

THE FIFTH C—
COORDINATION OF
INTELLIGENCE

Chapter Twenty

Negotiation Is about Teamwork (Attempted Suicide)

Crisis negotiator Ken Fung (Kuen)

In a negotiation, a negotiator relies very much on his team members to feed him timely information and give him support. Every member's role is crucial.

Early one morning, a man in his sixties bashed his wife, causing serious injuries to her head. She was his wife by second marriage. Their teenage daughter dialled 999. An ambulance soon arrived. The daughter accompanied her injured mother to the hospital.

Prior to police arrival, the husband had climbed through a window at his home and stood on a ledge on the outer wall of the public housing building, many floors above the ground. He refused to surrender himself to police.

The police requested that the Police Negotiation Cadre (PNC) attend the scene. The fire services had laid out a rescue cushion on the ground. They were also getting ready to conduct a high-angle rescue.

Ken Fung joined the PNC in 2015. He was a sergeant at the time of handling the incident. Two very experienced PNC members had arrived, and one of them was talking to the man. Ken and other PNC members provided support and spoke to the man's family to obtain more information.

Ken talked to the eldest son from the man's first marriage. His father and stepmother got married in China and had two daughters. The stepmother and the children resided in China. After some years, she and their children were granted resident-ship to join her husband in Hong Kong. The eldest son then moved out from his father's home.

About a month or so ago, his father and stepmother had a dispute at home. The wife made a police report accusing her husband of assaulting her. The police arrested the man. The case resulted in a binding over order in the magistrate's court.

Since then, the man had convinced himself that his wife had been scheming to take his money and property. He also sus-pected that his wife provoke him into arguments with the ul-timate intention of evicting him from the public housing flat, whose title was in his name. To his way of thinking, not only would his wife succeed in gaining residence in Hong Kong, but she could also live in the public housing flat with their two teenage daughters. She would fulfil her long-held Hong Kong dream.

The man felt that he had been deceived into marrying the sec-ond wife and was greatly wronged. He told his son repeatedly that he would die with his wife rather than let her take away everything he had. Of late, the man began transferring his as-sets to his eldest son. He also wished his son to take over his business in China. To Ken, this information set off alarm bells. The fact that he was in the process of transferring his funds to his son was a sign of the seriousness of his intent. There was a distinct possibility that he would indeed take his own life and that of his wife.

Meanwhile, the man told the negotiator to fetch his eldest son. He wanted to talk to him. *He has not killed himself yet. What is stopping the man from jumping? What is holding him back?* Ken pondered.

The eldest son arrived at the scene. The negotiator relayed to the man that his eldest son was at the scene and was very concerned for his safety. He suggested the man go back into the flat, and he would be able to talk to his son. The man did not respond. A while later, the man took out his mobile phone, contacted someone, and began talking in a hushed voice. He chose to ignore the negotiator.

The negotiator requested Ken and his teammates find out the identity of the person to whom the man was talking over the phone. The PNC team frantically checked with all the relatives at the scene. Nobody was engaged in any conversation with the man. They contacted the police officers, who accompanied the man's wife to the hospital. They replied that nobody was on the phone.

Ken decided to race to the hospital to verify the situation himself. Inside a waiting room at the hospital, Ken saw the man's daughter on the phone talking to her father. Very firmly and politely, Ken told the girl to hang up right away. He then asked the girl to tell him what they were talking about.

'Pa Pa kept asking me how Ma Ma's condition was. He asked me to tell Ma that he would forgive her for what she had done to him. He kept asking whether Ma had died or not. I told him I don't know yet,' the girl replied.

When the man could no longer talk to the daughter, he turned his attention back to the negotiator. He told the negotiator that once he knew that his wife would be OK, he would surrender.

However, from what Ken learned from the man's eldest son, the man might not really wish that his wife survived her injuries. If his wife died, she would not be able to take away his assets. He might then end his own life once that worry evaporated. Thus, the man might be pretending to care about his wife's well-being in order to get first-hand information about whether or not she had survived.

Ken informed the negotiator not to disclose the woman's actual status and to emphasise two points when he talked with the man.

The negotiator followed Ken's advice and said to the man, 'All I know is that the doctors are trying their best to save your wife. We do not know whether she can pull through or not. You wish your son to take over your business. How could you be certain that your relatives will not deceive your son and swindle all your money if you are not around anymore? You well know that business on the mainland depends very much on networking and knowing the right people. You have not introduced your son to all your business associates yet.' The negotiator stressed the two points to the man. First, his wife was still alive up to that point. Second, he highlighted the risk of leaving his son to take over the business without him there. The negotiator let those words sink in. He had created a dilemma in the man's mind. Soon after, the man surrendered. The firemen secured him with a harness and brought him to safety. He was arrested and charged with critically wounding his wife.

Ken's reflection

This case demonstrated the importance of teamwork in a negotiation process. When the negotiator noticed that the man was talking on the phone, he immediately asked his PNC team to find out to whom the man was talking to. As long as the man kept talking over the phone, he would not respond to the negotiator. Such a disruption was dangerous because the negotiator would not know what the man's plan might be.

The PNC team had to put a stop to the telephone conversation. When Ken contacted the police colleague to find out information for him, he received the reply that no relatives at the hospital were on the phone. In the end, he decided to race to the hospital to check the situation out personally. He was glad that he took that step and was able to stop the daughter from feeding information to her father.

After collating and analysing all relevant information, Ken advised the negotiator what to say to the man. The two pieces of information became the hook and were instrumental in persuading the man to abort his suicide attempt.

Coordination of Intelligence

The PNC teammates made enquiries with the man's family, collected information and analysed it, and fed relevant intelligence to the negotiator to facilitate the negotiation process. It is a good example of intelligence-led negotiation.

Chapter Twenty-One

Talking to a Murderer (Barricade)

Crisis negotiators Edwin Lui and Gilbert Wong

This case left an indelible memory on all the personnel who were involved in handling it, irrespective of the roles in which they were engaged.

Early in the evening on 20 December 2002, a thirty-eight-year-old man barricaded himself and his three young children inside his two-storey house in Pak Sha Village, Yuen Long, the New Territories. He called his niece to demand that his twenty-two-year-old wife come home. If his wife did not show up, he would kill himself and their children. The niece made a report. The police who responded to the scene immediately requested that the Police Negotiation Cadre (PNC) attend the scene.

Gilbert Wong and Edwin Lui completed their crisis negotiation training together in 1999. At the time of this incident, both were senior inspectors of police. They and two other PNC members handled the negotiation.

The background information revealed that the man was a Vietnamese Chinese. He had settled in Hong Kong long ago. He had rented an old-style two-storey village house in Pak Sha Village several years ago. He had courted his current wife when she was eleven years old and married her when she turned fourteen. They had one boy and two girls, all under five years old.

The PNC team arrived at the ground floor of the village house. The man refused to open the door or show his face. Edwin took up the role of negotiator, with Gilbert as his partner to offer support and assistance. On the ground floor, Edwin shouted, 'Hey, man, I know something has happened. I hope to resolve this incident peacefully. I do not wish any unhappy things to occur or anyone to get hurt. What has caused you to lock yourself in with your children? We can work out a solution.'

The man said he loved his wife and had worked hard to be a responsible breadwinner. About a week or so ago, his wife suddenly left home, and he had no news of her whereabouts. He made enquiries with her family and friends, but to no avail. That day, he called his niece in order to relay a message to his wife. He demanded that his wife come home. He had bought two cans of LPG gas and would blow up the house if she did not show up. The man did not demonstrate much anger or agitation when he talked. Edwin felt more unsettled. This lack of emotion was a cause for real concern.

'Listen carefully. Tell that woman to come here. I need to ask her. If she wants custody of the three kids, come and get them. She can have the children. I'll take my own life. If she leaves the kids with me, that is fine with me. When I kill myself, I will take them along. I give you thirty minutes. The countdown starts now,' the man spoke in a resolute tone. Edwin tried to suggest alternatives to resolve the situation and asked about the well-being of the children.

'They are still safe and sound. But somebody is not. A girl, her classmate, came here to play with my daughter. Well, she's in the cupboard now. I killed her. The corpse is in the cupboard.'

Edwin listened with shock to the cold-hearted confession. If it turned out to be true, he was talking to a murderer. The man's voice was so calm, so level. What was most chilling was that he spoke about the murder as if he was engaged in a mundane, everyday-conversation.

Edwin tried to give the impression that he was not overly shocked by the confession. He did not want to press the man too far on the matter. However, he did try to find out more about what had happened.

'Uh, you killed a girl? What was she doing in your home? Did she annoy you in some way? Are you just kidding?' While the negotiator talked to the man, he recalled that two young girls, aged around eleven, had been reported missing in the last two weeks. They resided in the same village and were unrelated to each other. They were reported missing after leaving home on errands. *If the man confessed that he had killed one girl, might he also be responsible for the disappearance of the other one?* Edwin contemplated.

'Do I sound like I'm bluffing?' the man replied. While they continued talking about the dead girl and other matters, the man said, 'Eh, thirty minutes is up. Where is my wife? Has she arrived yet? Don't play games with me.' Not long after, sounds of nails being hammered into a wooden board could be heard from inside the house. It was later revealed that the man had placed a wooden board horizontally on the top of the staircase leading up to the first floor. He had intended to hinder the police's access to the first floor.

The PNC support team and the police incident commander assessed the situation. There was no positive progress in the negotiation. The man had not budged an inch. They had a grim feeling that the man was going to blow up the house soon. Time was of the essence. The incident commander decided to make a forced entry.

Meanwhile, Edwin guided the wife's sister to engage in conversation with the man. It was hoped that she would be able to persuade him to surrender. Edwin had put on a fire-resistant tunic that was borrowed from the fire services. It was to protect him in case an explosion occurred. Edwin informed the firemen that there might be a girl's dead body inside a cupboard.

When the firemen were about to break down the door, a sudden, loud explosion occurred, startling everyone. This was followed by fire gushing out of a window on the first floor. They had no time to lose. The firemen broke the door and gained entry.

They pushed through the broken wooden board barrier on the top of the stairs. The firemen found the man and his three children on the first floor, all seriously injured by the explosion. The man had ignited two cans of LPG gas. 'One dead body inside a cupboard!' Edwin heard a fireman shout out.

The incident lasted over three hours. It was already dark when the operation finished. The man and his three children were rescued and taken to the hospital. The house and its immediate vicinity were cordoned off and put under police guard.

The incident made front-page news in all the local newspapers and was widely covered in subsequent issues.

On the day after the incident, the police detectives returned to the scene to conduct a thorough search. A manhole at the back of the house aroused suspicion. The cement that sealed the opening of the manhole appeared to be laid quite recently. An old air-conditioner was put on top of it. The cement was removed. At the bottom of the seven feet deep manhole was a dead body floating in four feet of muddy water. The fire services' divers took over four hours to retrieve the dead body.

The two dead bodies were confirmed to be those of the two girls who had been previously reported as missing. The man and his three children survived, although they had severe burns to their faces and bodies. The man was arrested and subsequently charged with all the heinous crimes he had committed. On 25 February 2004, he was convicted in the Court of First Instance for the double murder and attempted murder of his three children. He was sentenced to life imprisonment (South China Morning Post, 2004 February 26, *Double Life Sentence of Killer of Schoolgirls*).

Hong Kong is renowned for being a safe place to live. The double murder was a big shock to the people of Hong Kong at that time.

Reflection by Edwin and Gilbert

When Edwin and Gilbert were negotiating with the man, the notion of him being a murderer had never crossed their minds. When they finally knew that they had been talking to a murderer all that time, the knowledge chilled them to the bone. The man was so calm and in control of his emotions that it was very difficult to form the notion that he was capable of such cold-blooded murders.

This case was a horrific example of domestic violence. The man had courted his young wife when she was only eleven years old and married her when she was just a teenager. They had an age gap of more than fifteen years. The foundation of their marriage was insecure from the start. From the interaction, the man appeared to be possessive and a control freak. He could not stand his wife leaving the family and eventually chose to pursue a tragic course and wreak vengeance on her.

They felt very sorry for the couple's three children, who were injured in the explosion. Not only had they have to live through the trauma of the incident, but they would also know in time that their father was a convicted murderer of two young girls. A classmate of one daughter was amongst the victims. It must have been a long road to recovery for them, their mother, and the families of the two deceased girls.

Authors' note

The children should be in their late teens to early twenties by the time Edwin and Gilbert shared this story. All of us sincerely wish them well and hope they have coped with life.

The incident made headlines in the news at that time, so it would not be difficult to identify the exact date of this incident. Therefore, the exact date of the incident was included in this article.

Coordination of Intelligence

The man was uncooperative from the beginning. With three young children's lives at stake, the police incident commander, the tactical team, the PNC team, and the fire services worked closely together to work out a rescue plan.

All the information collected from the wife, the niece, and the neighbours helped build an understanding of the family background. When Edwin heard the man's confession about the murder of the young girl, he immediately thought about the two missing girls reported missing in Yuen Long. He forewarned the firemen about a possible dead body in the house. The discovery of one dead body led to further enquiry and detection of the second murder. The coordination of intelligence amongst the stakeholders effectively saved the lives of three children and helped bring closure for the families of the two missing girls.

Chapter Twenty-Two

Father and Mother's Tug of War (Barricade)

Crisis negotiator Stephen Liauw

A child's arrival can bring wonder and joy to parents. However, when one child is followed quickly by another child, unexpected and troublesome situations may arise. Parents will invariably face a daunting task when they need to look after several young children close in age.

Consider the scene of a father and mother working together to change a baby's diaper. An admirable display of loving parenting? Maybe not. Maybe it is a tug of war?

On a summer evening, the police received a report that a man had barricaded himself inside his home in Ngau Tau Kok, Kowloon. He was holding his ten-month-old baby captive. The young couple had five very young children.

On that day, the couple argued. Shaken by her husband's hot temper and threat to harm her and the children, the wife left home with all the children—except one. Her husband held on to the youngest baby and refused to let go. A report was made to the police.

The police requested that the Police Negotiation Cadre (PNC) attend the scene to defuse the crisis. A tactical team from the emergency unit, Kowloon East Region (EU KE) had already stationed itself outside the flat, ready to take orders from the police incident commander.

Stephen Liauw joined the PNC in 2006. He was an inspector of police at that time. The PNC team entered the flat. The man came out from the bedroom holding the baby and pointing a knife at his neck. Stephen initiated a dialogue. His PNC teammate had left the flat briefly to coordinate some logistics. Because Stephen was on his own, he began jotting down information on his notepad. His head was slightly bowed when he heard a mocking sigh.

'Eh, young man, you are taking notes. New guy, eh? What now? Afraid you will miss out information and can't complete a report afterwards?' The man's biting remark caught him off guard.

Stephen nodded with a gentle smile on his face, stopped writing, and put aside his notepad. *I will make do with listening and remembering the crucial information for the time being*, he thought.

Stephen suggested the man put the baby to one side. The man immediately shouted, 'Don't you dare come near! I'll put the baby right here.' He put the baby against a wall and continued. 'Don't come near! If you push or touch me, you will be the one injuring the baby. You are to blame, not me! Step away!'

As the time passed, other negotiators came along and took turns talking to the man. Nearly three hours had gone by.

The man talked about the crazy life involved in looking after five young children. It was an exhausting, non-stop cycle of feeding, changing diapers, cooking, washing clothes, seeing them to bed, and completing many other chores. As time went by, the baby started crying and was hungry. The man was not prepared to put down the baby or his knife. He had no spare hand to prepare the milk.

'I can assist you to prepare the infant formula. You tell me what to do,' a negotiator suggested. The man nodded. He went into the kitchen and came out with a feeding bottle, a portion of infant formula, and water.

'Okay. Pour the infant formula into the feeding bottle, then the hot water, then cold water—yes, that's right. Now, shake it to mix it up.'

The negotiator followed the man's directions. He then squeezed some milk onto the man's hand as requested and asked, 'How's the temperature? Is it right for feeding the baby?'

'It's good, it's good. Put the bottle on the table. I'll get it.' The baby sucked on the nipple eagerly and stopped crying.

The negotiator watched the father feed and burp the baby. He looked gentle and fatherly at that moment. Still, he did not change his stance on his singular demand. He demanded that his wife come home with all the children. He said he would ask for her forgiveness.

According to the information being fed to the negotiator, his wife was too scared to come back. The negotiator suspected that the wife might have suffered some physical and verbal abuse over time.

As time ticked by, the situation remained in a stalemate. Midnight was approaching. After much discussion and a detailed risk assessment, the police incident commander decided to accede to the man's request.

The negotiator told the man that they would arrange a meeting between him and his wife at their home. As a gesture of good-will, the man agreed to surrender the knife and throw it to the floor. The negotiator picked it up and passed to the tactical team at the rear.

'One of our guys recalled the man carrying a small knife with a red blade. The one that the man surrendered did not have a red blade,' one police officer noted. This piece of information was passed to the negotiator, and he kept a mental note of it.

Inside the flat, the negotiator discussed with the man how and where he would sit when his wife arrived, the position of the negotiator, the distance between them, and all the other nec-essary preparations. Several times the man objected to the ar-rangement. He was concerned that the police would come near him and arrest him. The negotiator assured him repeatedly that they would not make any attempt to capture him or snatch the baby during the meeting.

It took over an hour for both sides to work out the details of the meeting. The man would sit on a sofa near the bedroom. The wife would sit on a chair opposite the man in an L-shape setting.

The negotiator made sure there was no obstacle between the woman and the main door. He and his team members would stand in between the L-shape setting. He would be within an arm's length to protect the woman in case of sudden, unfore-seen circumstances.

Outside the flat, the tactical team positioned themselves along the corridor. Each police officer knew what to do when called upon to take action. The team leader of the tactical team had an unobstructed view of the meeting and would give the order to take action if required.

Everyone was ready. The negotiator was notified that the wife was walking up the stairs. The building had no lift. The man had gone inside the bedroom with the baby. The negotiator invited the man to come out. He held the baby in his cradle. The man walked into the living room slowly and was about to sit down at the prearranged position.

'Stop! Everyone, hold!' At this unexpected command from the negotiator, the police officers outside knew what to do. It was part of the briefing beforehand, in case of any irregularity in the meeting arrangements. The wife was escorted back downstairs to the lobby. The tactical team was right at the door, ready to take action.

'What are you holding in your hand? I need to see it,' the negotiator said in a firm, steady voice. His eyes had caught a glimpse of something shiny. Something was hidden in the man's hand. After a pause, the man threw a small knife with a red blade to the floor a few steps in front of him.

The negotiator had seen a similar type of knife before. They are sometimes attached to some martial arts cartoon magazines as gifts, meant to attract buyers' interest. *This knife is not exactly a lethal weapon, but why did he hide such thing in his palm? That must've been the knife that the police officer saw earlier on*, he thought with relief. He made a mental note, after all this was over, to thank that officer for his keen observation.

The negotiator and his partner spoke to the man in a serious tone, pointing out that he had betrayed their trust. However, they did not wish to overwhelm him with a sense of blame. 'Just one more step! One step. We can do this together. You will be able to see your wife,' the negotiator urged the man. Eventually, the man agreed to cooperate fully with the negotiator. The meeting resumed. The man sat on the sofa. The wife entered the flat and sat opposite him, as agreed upon earlier.

The man spoke first. 'I hope that you will come back home with the kids. I am sorry for losing my temper. Will you forgive me?' he said calmly.

'I—I forgive you,' the wife replied timidly. She could not bring herself to look directly at her husband. Her eyes were anchored on her baby.

'Will you come home?'

'Yes, as you wish. Whatever you wish,' she stuttered nervously. 'I think our baby's diaper needs changing. Can—can you fetch a clean one and some cleaning cotton?'

'Uh, I'll get them.' The man went into the bedroom and emerged shortly afterwards with a bag of clean diapers.

The negotiator and his partner kept a close watch. The parents changed the baby's diaper in the father's arms. The father's hands were glued to the baby. Their hands criss-crossed over the diaper changing. At a superficial level, their action could be construed as being gentle, even affectionate.

Yet it was plain to see that beneath these seemingly loving gestures, a battle was being fought between two polarised forces, each wishing to own this particular moment, this particular child. In every sense, this couple were rivals. The father was desperate and possessive. The mother was passionate and protective.

To the shock of those who were witnessing this scene, the mother did something extraordinary. Without any warning, she grabbed the baby, turned towards the door, and rushed out.

Everything happened at once and in quick succession. The man struggled in a feeble protest. The PNC members intervened immediately to subdue the man. The woman was whisked away with the baby safe in her arms. The tactical team closed in to handle the man. It had taken over nine hours to defuse the crisis.

Authors' note

The date of the incident, exact family composition, and gender and age of the children are not disclosed in the story, to protect the identity of all the family members.

Stephen's reflection

Fresh out of crisis negotiation training, Stephen was still a rookie at the time that he handled this incident. This difficult case was a valuable learning experience.

First, doing things by the book does not always work. A negotiator needs to adapt what he/she has learned in the classroom to fit the real-life scenario. In training, negotiators are taught that when they talk to the subject, a partner will stay close by their side to jot down important information in a notebook and pass them to the PNC team to work out a strategy and negotiation plan.

In this case, the negotiator's partner had gone away temporarily, Stephen automatically took up his partner's role to jot down notes, which he thought was a normal step. He did not expect that would make him look unprofessional. Upon hearing the mocking comment from the subject person, he realised the impracticability of doing so. If he jotted notes while talking to the man, their communication would look like an interview rather than a dialogue. Therefore he immediately ceased taking notes and focused on talking to the man.

The negotiation went on for hours and seemed to be going in circles. Stephen's mind was full of questions, particularly what he would say and do next, given that he had nearly exhausted all the strategies he had been taught to implement.

At some stage, the man looked sleepy. Stephen was unsure whether he should invite the man to take a nap. He was wary that if he allowed the man to rest, it would simply give him renewed energy to prolong the crisis. He wondered how much longer the negotiation would take.

He was very grateful for the keen observation of the police officer who noticed that the knife which the man first surrendered was different from the one he had first displayed. The red blade knife was a toy at best, but it had a sharp end. The man must have some ulterior motive, or he would not have tried to hide it in the first place. Might he wish to threaten to harm himself or his wife if the course of events did not proceed well? In any case, Stephen did not ask the man why he hid that knife.

During the preparation stage of the meeting between the man and his wife, the PNC team had briefed the wife carefully about what to do and what to say. Her sudden act of snatching the baby was not in the plan. They were all caught by surprise when she did that without forewarning. Nevertheless, the PNC team and the tactical team were well prepared to respond to unforeseen circumstances and sudden emergencies. When the man tried to run after his fleeing wife and the baby, the PNC team blocked his way, and the tactical team closed in on him almost immediately. The man looked exhausted and defeated.

Stephen hoped that the couple would seek help after that incident. They must had been overwhelmed by the pressure of having to look after five very young kids.

Coordination of Intelligence

A great deal of intelligence collation had taken place in the background to find information that could be used by the negotiator in order to engage the man in active listening. Again, the PNC team leader regularly provided updates to the police incident commander so he/she was able to modify the decision-making.

The coordination of intelligence to the negotiator proved particularly important, especially with respect to possible weapons being carried by the man. The whole process of the meeting between the man and his wife was a successful operation carried out under the effective command of the incident commander.

Chapter Twenty-Three

Hijacking at the Hong Kong International Airport (Hostage-Taking)

Crisis negotiator Wilbut Chan

In Hong Kong's aviation history, were you aware of any aeroplane being hijacked? You may find details on the Internet about one which occurred in 1948 (Transport Security International, 2018 June 23, *The Legacy of the 'Miss Macao' Hijack: 70 Years On*). Fifty-two years later, in July 2000, another hijacking incident happened at the Hong Kong Chap Lap Kok International Airport. This airport was opened in 1998 and replaced the Kai Tak International Airport. The Police Negotiation Cadre (PNC) played a major role in resolving the crisis. The drama ended peacefully and without any casualties.

On 31 July 2000, shortly after ten in the evening, a Cathay Pacific commercial plane was being serviced at parking bay number twenty-nine, on the tarmac of the Hong Kong International Airport, before its scheduled departure to Paris later in the evening.

An Asian man in his late twenties rushed past the security control area and threatened the pursuing airport security staff with a pistol-like object. The man rushed into the Cathay Pacific commercial plane. There were no passengers on board. The police were informed.

'Help! Help! I beg you, let me go!' A female worker conducting cleaning services on the plane was paralysed with fear, as the man dragged her in and closed the door.

Wilbut Chan joined the PNC in 1999. He and two other members of the PNC were mobilised, and they arrived at the command centre in the airport shortly afterwards. Previously, officers of the airport security unit (ASU) were deployed in the vicinity of the plane and were ready to take action.

Inside the command centre, Wilbut dialled a mobile telephone number belonging to the cleaner. A frightened voice answered the call; she was the hostage. The hijacker took over the phone and talked nervously in broken English. He demanded that no police officers approach the plane. He demanded that the Hong Kong government arrange to fly him home. He claimed that he lived in a small village at the foot of the Himalayan Mountains. He had no travel documents with him.

Through some connected electronic devices, a team of police clinical psychologists (PCP) listened in to the live conversation with the intention of forming an opinion about the hijacker's frame of mind. The man did not mention anything about his family, but the PCP gathered from the hijacker's talk that he had family members faraway and missed them very much. They believed that he was acting alone. It was, in all probability, not an organised act of terrorism. Advised by the PCP, the negotiator focused his conversation upon the man's homeland and family. The PNC's empathetic attitude softened the man's stance.

Eventually, the hijacker accepted the negotiator's advice to turn himself in. This was a critical moment. On the one hand, the negotiator had to inform the tactical team that the man intended to surrender and detail how he would come out. The airport security unit took up the role of the tactical team in this incident. On the other hand, the negotiator had to guide the man, step by step, on how to surrender. Any sudden or unplanned movement by the hijacker might send a wrong signal to the tactical team, and he might be shot.

First, the hijacker was instructed to free the hostage and let her leave the plane. The man was told to leave the gun or any other weapon he might have on the floor of the aircraft. He walked out of the plane very slowly, with hands raised and palms facing outwards, indicating he was not carrying anything. The tactical team rushed forward and arrested him.

A thorough search on the Internet did not reveal details about this hijacking incident on that exact date, 31 July 2000. However, an article from the *South China Morning Post* reported the plight of the hijacker (South China Morning Post, 2004 December 24, *Hijack Drama Mystery Man in Diplomatic Limbo*). In February 2001, the man pleaded guilty to carrying an imitation firearm with intent to commit a crime and having detained the cleaner unlawfully. He was sentenced to five years' imprisonment. Upon his discharge from prison in December 2004, the Hong Kong immigration authorities still could not authenticate his nationality claim. They believed that the man did not reveal the complete story of his unauthorised entry into Hong Kong.

Wilbut's reflection

This call-out was a highly unusual assignment. On his way to the airport, many issues popped up in his mind as he collected intelligence with the police officers at the scene over the phone and formulated his negotiation plan. In the initial stages, limited information was known about the hijacker. Having considered that much crucial information was yet to be ascertained (such as the type and number of weapon the hijacker might be carrying), it would be too dangerous to approach him at close distance. The PNC team decided to talk to the hijacker over the phone.

The fact that the drama was concluded peacefully, in a relatively short period, and without casualty was not simply a case of good luck or chance. Wilbut was grateful for the assistance and support given to him by all the stakeholders in the background during that time. (Note: According to the *Sing Tao Daily News* dated 2 August 2000, the negotiation talk commenced at 2355 hours and concluded at 0040 hours.)

Coordination of Intelligence

A plane hijacking is a very serious incident. Based on the authors' years of experience working in the Hong Kong police, it is not difficult to imagine that a multitude of government department personnel must have been mobilised to man the centralised command and control centre. Many units and much manpower must have been at work to find out anything and everything about the hijacker. Was it a planned act? Were there accomplices? If so, who were they and where were they? As for a plan, there would need to be a systematic division of labour. There would be floor plans, whiteboards, dedicated telephone lines, briefing rooms, log books—the list goes on.

Useful and timely intelligence was passed on to the negotiator to facilitate his negotiation. This intervention was a demonstration of coordination of intelligence at its finest. The crisis negotiators' declaration fits this scenario to perfection:

Where there is a crisis, let us negotiate to bring resolution;
Where hostages have been taken, let us negotiate to bring safety;
Where there is terror, let us negotiate to bring peace ...

A painting, 'Beacon', by Karma Castilho.

This art work portrays a dense woodland. The woodland is not healthy. The depletion of sunlight has caused the branches to wither. How quickly the sombre mood of the painting changes when a beacon of light penetrates the dimness. Where this light shines, trees and shrubs embrace the opportunity to grow and blossom.

This painting is a metaphor for the situation where the police negotiator penetrates the seemingly endless darkness which has enveloped the troubled soul. The negotiator is a beacon of hope, illuminating within the troubled person the possibility that there is an alternative to hopelessness and despair, and that life can be good once more.

Part G:

THE SIXTH C—CARE

Chapter Twenty-Four

Every Cloud Has
a Silver Lining
(Attempted Suicide)

Crisis negotiator Calvin Cheung

When unpleasant experiences cloud a person's life journey, that person sees only mist and darkness ahead. He/she contemplates suicide. Then, someone offers an ear. Slowly but surely, that person finds hope.

On a summer morning in 2006, a man in his mid-forties sought treatment for his injured leg at the casualty department of a government hospital in the New Territories, Hong Kong. During a consultation, the attending doctor observed that the man displayed symptoms of psychosis. The man became hostile and agitated upon hearing that the doctor would not admit him and would instead transfer him to a psychiatric hospital. He left the consultation room abruptly and rushed to the rooftop. The man sat on a ledge on the outer wall of the hospital building and threatened to jump if anybody approached him.

The police were called, and they requested the Police Negotiation Cadre (PNC) attend the scene, in order to defuse the crisis.

Calvin Cheung joined the PNC in July 2006. He had just completed his two-week crisis negotiation training. He and a group of newly graduated PNC members followed the on-call PNC team to attend the scene. He was a police constable when he handled this incident.

According to the information collected by the uniformed police officers, the man had just been discharged from prison and was a drug addict. The experienced negotiators, accompanied by a few trainees, took turns talking to the man. The man was not too responsive at first, but he gradually became a little more communicative.

Calvin made an attempt to draw the man out in his conversation. Little by little, the man opened up. 'After primary six [equivalent to grade six], I stopped schooling. I did odd jobs here and there. Then I couldn't find a job. I got into drugs. I needed money. I was caught doing that thing—you know. When I was in prison, none of my friends visited me. Ah Hing and a few others, they used to call me big brother. When I got into prison, everybody disappeared.' He scoffed and continued. 'My mom visited me in prison. She scolded and lectured me all the time. Sometimes I couldn't stand it and shouted at her to shut up or go away. But this crazy old woman came to visit me again and again.'

It had taken quite some time for the man to reveal this much about himself. The negotiator listened patiently. He nodded occasionally and acknowledged the man's despondency. 'Your mother visited you in prison. I think your mother cares about you very much. You care a lot about her too,' he responded with empathy.

'No one listens to me the way you do.' The man sighed and took a deep breath. 'I hate going to psychiatric hospitals. People think I am really crazy, but I'm not! Sometimes I don't know what I'm doing when I'm a bit high.'

'Um, I understand. It is not an easy life that you have gone through,' the negotiator comforted him. From being in a down-cast and slumped position, the man straightened up a little bit and looked up into the sky. The negotiator sensed that the man was ready for the next move. 'Let us help you. You are very brave in taking this step to come back in. Stay where you are. You need to sit still and hold onto the railing. The firemen will come and help you. You are doing very well.' The negotiator spoke slowly and gently. Meanwhile, the firemen secured the man with a harness before moving him back to a safe place.

The ambulance men put the man on a stretcher to take him down to the ground floor. They told him that he would be con-veyed to a psychiatric hospital. He did not protest.

The man made a signal to the ambulance men to stop when he was passing by the negotiator. 'Sir, thank you for talking to me. I—I'll treasure my life. Thank you.' While saying that, the man reached out his hand.

Calvin held the man's hand firmly, looked into his eyes, and replied warmly, 'Take good care of yourself and your mother.'

Calvin's reflection

This case was Calvin's first case after he completed his crisis negotiation training. He treasured the opportunity to be able to observe other more experienced PNC members at work. When he was given the opportunity to be the negotiator at hand, he was glad and somewhat relieved that over time, the man was prepared to accept the sincerity and integrity of what he had to say and suggest.

Care

The man was at a low point in his life. During his imprisonment, his friends distanced themselves from him. He realised they were not his true friends after all. The negotiator listened to him patiently and acknowledged the sadness and disappointment he felt at the time. The negotiator's sincerity touched him. The man felt that someone cared about his well-being. His mindset was changed, and he aborted the suicide attempt.

Chapter Twenty-Five

Talking on the Same Wavelength (Attempted Suicide)

Crisis negotiator Edwin Lui

How do you find a person's favourite subjects to engage her/him in a dialogue? In this incident, a negotiator strikes a respondent chord with a man threatening suicide, using their mutual interest in art.

Edwin Lui joined the Police Negotiation Cadre (PNC) in 1999 and remained a member until his retirement in 2012. He was a senior inspector of police when he handled this incident. On the way to work on a summer morning in 2002, Edwin had to make a detour. He arrived at the rooftop of a ten-storey tenement. A man in his late forties was sitting on a metal shack on the roof.

'Morning, mister. Someone saw you sitting there and was concerned for your safety. Police notified me to come here. Can I talk to you?' Edwin greeted the man.

The man had climbed onto the top of the shack and was sitting on the edge, with his feet dangling in the air. 'Stay where you are. Don't come near. I'll jump if you walk a step closer,' he said.

'I'll do as you say and won't come near you. So, you live here? I mean the premises underneath you. You mind if I take a look?' the negotiator asked the man, who made a welcoming gesture.

Inside the shack, the furnishing was sparse but neatly arranged. Several paintings were hung on the wall. The negotiator came out to sit on a raised platform a small distance away from the shack. From here he could see the man.

'You have hung quite a few watercolour paintings on the wall. They are lovely. The poems by the side of the paintings aptly describe the scenery. One can easily get carried away by the magic of the scenic world. Who drew them? Did you draw them?'

'I am up here on my own a lot. I like doing some painting when I'm in the mood. I add a poem to it sometimes. I'm very much on my own, ever since my wife passed away. There is nobody worth talking to. The paintings and the poems are my best companions.'

'That painting, *Sunrise on the Lantau Peak*, is the second highest mountain in Hong Kong. You've captured a most beautiful wonder of nature. I admire your talent. Did you do a live drawing there, or did you draw it from a photograph? What motivated you to draw this scenery? Can you tell me more?'

The man was delighted to have a listener. Their conversation extended to the appreciation of classical Chinese poems and essays. The negotiator recited a few classical poems that befitted the atmosphere.

After observing that the man's mood had lightened up, the negotiator suggested, 'You have a good view from where you are sitting. You may feel it's nothing, but it looks quite dangerous. I feel uncomfortable talking to you like this, because I am concerned for your safety. Can you walk back a bit? You are such a learned scholar. I would very much like to hear more about your appreciation of the Chinese poems. No need to hurry. Come down step by step.'

The man got up and walked a few steps towards the negotiator. Without warning, the man went down on his knees and into a prostrate position. He said, 'I admire you with awe and reverence.'

'Hey, friend, this is too much! Let me help you.' Edwin approached the man and helped him to his feet. He advised the man the location of some recreational centres in the neighbourhood. The incident ended peacefully.

Edwin's reflection

Loneliness can be both physical and spiritual. An intellectual like the man in this case sees worldly matters from a poetic and artistic perspective. He probably had little social contact with neighbours or friends. Having lost the love of his life, lacking in interpersonal skills, and unable to find social support, the man's loneliness weighed down on him. He became depressed and found life meaningless.

Edwin was glad that he was able to appreciate the man's artistic excellence. However, the man's response was unexpected. That pleasant experience has stayed with him for all these years.

Care

The negotiator took the time to visit the man's living place, acknowledge and appreciate his world and talents, and empathise with his loneliness. The negotiator's care genuinely touched the man. His mood lifted, and he agreed to go back to a safe place.

Chapter Twenty-Six

The Best-Laid Plans of Mice and Men (Attempted Suicide)

Crisis negotiator Ricky Tsang

In Hong Kong, there are often stories about parents working hard to save up money not for themselves but for the welfare of their children. The money is for their children to get married and buy a flat. Moreover, they willingly put their children's name down as the only rightful owner of that flat. 'The flat will be passed on to our child when we pass away anyway, so why not save the administrative cost of having to change the ownership of the flat to the child later?' Many parents think this way.

In this scenario, a man was about to lose half of the ownership of his flat to his estranged wife. The flat was paid for with his aged parents' life savings. Unable to face such bleak consequences, he wished to end his misery by taking his own life. A police negotiator intervened, and through empathetic listening, the man found renewed reason to embrace life rather than death at his own hand.

Around 1.00 a.m. on a day in 2015, the police received a report that a man in his late thirties was standing on a concrete cover on the top of an air-conditioning unit on the outer wall of a building, many storeys above the ground in Kowloon.

The fire services surveyed the building. Because of a platform on the first-floor podium, the firemen were unable to inflate and position the rescue cushion on the first floor to break the man's fall should he jump.

Ricky Tsang had just completed his training in crisis negotiation and joined the Police Negotiation Cadre (PNC) in 2015. He was a station sergeant at the time of handling the incident. The police requested that the PNC attend the scene to defuse the crisis.

When Ricky and the PNC team arrived at the flat, the man's aged parents were there. They were in their late seventies. Silent tears rolled down the old lady's face. The elderly father walked rest-lessly to and fro, feeling lost and helpless. They did not display any anger towards their son at all.

The man's friend had also arrived at the scene, to provide as-sistance. The three of them provided the following background information. The man lived with his aged parents at the flat. He earned a meagre income. Years ago, his parents had pur-chased this government-subsidised flat under a home owner-ship scheme.

A picture of the same type of government-subsidised building mentioned in this scenario. The circle indicates the approximate location where the man positioned himself (it was not the actual unit in this scenario). It was taken in 2018 during the writing of this book.

The Home Ownership Scheme (HOS) is a subsidised sale pro-gramme of public housing flats in Hong Kong initiated by the Hong Kong Government since the late 1970s. The scheme pro-vides an opportunity for home ownership for lower to middle income families who cannot afford to buy flat in the private sector. (The Hong Kong Housing Authority, *Home Ownership*. Wikipedia, *Home Ownership Scheme*).

The parents put their life savings together to pay for the down payment, and they covered the monthly mortgage payment. Without hesitation, they put the ownership of the HOS flat under their son's name. Several years ago, the son dated a woman, and they were married. The couple lived with their parents in the flat. The parents were happy to see that their only son had the security of a permanent home and was married.

About a year ago, their daughter-in-law suddenly moved out. Then a month ago, the son received a letter from a solicitor who was representing his wife. The wife wished to file for divorce. She also intended to request alimony and claim her rightful share of her husband's property. Because the flat was in the son's name, his wife was entitled to have an equal share of the property should they get divorced.

The son was devastated by the failed marriage. Moreover, he felt greatly indebted to his aged parents, who had sacrificed so much to give him a good home and life. The flat belonged to his parents because they had paid for it. Feeling guilt-ridden, he confided in his friend and had been drinking heavily for the last few nights.

The man had climbed through the kitchen window, hung onto a drainage pipe, and stepped on the ledge in order to reach the concrete top cover of an air-conditioning unit.

Ricky, the negotiator, wore a harness provided by the fire services because he had to lean his body more than halfway out of a kitchen window to establish eye contact with the man.

A picture of a ledge of the type of government-subsidised building depicted in this scenario. The arrow indicates how the man possibly climbed out of a kitchen window and reached the top cover of an air-conditioning unit (it was not the actual unit in this scenario). It was taken in 2018 during the writing of this book.

'Hello, man. You look very unhappy. I am here to offer help. Can you tell me what happened?'

At first the man was reluctant to talk. He looked down at times. 'Look this way, please, over here. Look at me. You can tell me the reasons that have made you so depressed. We can face the problems together. You don't have to shoulder them all on your ow,' Ricky took his time to say those words in a sincere tone.

From the incoherent, abrupt utterances of the man, Ricky suspected that the man was under the influence of alcohol. It would take some time for him to sober up.

Some time passed. Gradually, the man opened up and talked about his feelings of guilt and how he thought that he had betrayed his parents' good intentions for him. 'They have worked so hard all their lives. The flat, it is not my flat. They put in all their hard-earned money. Everything they have done is for me and me only. Look at me. I'm a total failure. My parents have sacrificed so much for me. Very soon, they will have no place to live. It is because of what I have done. How I wish I had not married that woman. Now, she will take away half of everything I have. But this flat belongs to my parents! How could I ever repay their unconditional love for me?'

'I appreciate you sharing all this with me. It is not easy to do so. Your parents wish me to tell you that they are not angry with you. They are anxious about you. The most important thing is that you are safe.' Ricky maintained a supportive and reassuring tone. In time, the man calmed down and stopped talking about jumping to his death. The PNC team considered it worth a try to start the rescue. The fire services prepared to conduct a high-angle rescue.

'We can face the problem together. You remain where you are and stay calm. There is no need to move. A fireman will come down to you from above and secure you with a harness. He will bring you back to safety. The fireman is coming down now.'

The man did not put up any resistance. Ricky continued. 'You are doing very well. You have made a correct decision to allow the fireman to approach you. Now he will put a harness around you and pull you up.'

The man was brought back to safety. The negotiator accompanied the man to meet his parents. It was a very touching reunion. The son was full of remorse. The parents were accommodating and forgiving.

The old lady turned to Ricky, gave him a warm hug, and said, 'Sir, you have saved my son's life. I can't thank you enough.' She turned to her son and continued. 'Money is only a worldly possession, not important. You are most important, son. Don't ever do such a thing again.' Tears streamed down her face as she hugged her son.

'Mister, can you promise your mother that you will never do such a thing again? Can you do that? Look at them. They are so old. You need to look after them.'

'Ma Ma and Pa Pa, I am so sorry. I promise. I promise.' The man sobbed as he made the promise.

Ricky's reflection

When Ricky learned what drove the man towards wishing to end his own life, he empathised with his predicament. His parents had done a lot to ensure that their only child could be well provided for when they passed away. The man might have lived in a protected environment, nurtured by his parents all his life. When his marriage did not work out and he faced a future of having to lose half of what his parents had built up for him, he found the impasse too much to cope with and went into crisis mode.

Through active listening, the man was given time and space to express his profound misery. In time, he came to his senses and realised that life and his parents' love were worth more than the loss of his flat.

Care

The man's wish to die stemmed from a great indebtedness that he felt towards his aged parents. He was a good man at heart and loved his parents. Therefore, once the negotiator showed him that his parents cared and loved him more than the money that his son would lose, the man was able to reclaim his sense of balance and will to live.

As a saying goes, 'The best-laid plans of mice and men often go awry.' No matter how well a plan that the parents had worked out for their son, things could still go wrong when one least expected it.

Chapter Twenty-Seven

Every Child Deserves a Childhood; Every Child Is Entitled to an Education (Attempted Suicide)

Crisis negotiator Calvin Cheung

Occasionally, some people come to Hong Kong to express their grievances about alleged injustices they have faced in their home country. This episode is about such a woman. She adopted an extreme form of expression by engaging in self-harm. Her eight-year-old daughter was her staunch ally. After a police negotiation team's intervention, the woman aborted the act. A police negotiator shares some thoughts about the mother-daughter relationship.

On an evening in mid-2018, a woman sat on an awning two floors above the ground, on the outer wall of a hotel in Yau Ma Tei, Kowloon. She reached that spot by climbing through the window inside a female washroom on the second floor of the hotel. She had hung a banner along the awning and was brandishing a cutter. She had also scattered flyers onto the floor. She had come to Hong Kong as a visitor. She was not staying at that hotel. Upon noticing that a crowd had gathered, the woman began a tirade against alleged unjust treatment by her country's government towards her and her family.

Calvin Cheung joined the Police Negotiation Cadre (PNC) in 2006. He was a chief inspector of police at the time of handling the incident.

When the PNC members arrived at the hotel, they wished to enter the female toilet, where the woman had climbed out to the awning. However, the woman's eight-year-old daughter blocked the door and said, 'Ma Ma forbade me to open the door. You can't enter.'

Not wanting to force their way in, the PNC team went to the floor immediately above. They managed to find a window in the common corridor on that floor. Calvin, the negotiator, shouted to the woman and let her know his location.

The woman had made a few superficial cuts on her arms with a cutter. She continued wailing and repeating her complaints. The negotiator listened and acknowledged her predicament. In time, he said to the woman, 'I understand your demands. We are a bit far apart. Can you ask your daughter to open the door of the toilet and let us come inside? In this way, we do not need to shout and can talk more comfortably. Please tell your daughter to open the door.'

After seeking permission from her mother, the girl opened the door to let the PNC members and uniformed police officers enter the toilet to continue their interaction. In time, the mother calmed down. Calvin promised her that he could inform the reporters about the nature of her grievances. He made it clear to her that he had no control over what the reporters would write. He also pointed out that due to the difference in jurisdiction, the Hong Kong police had no power to take action regarding her complaint.

The woman felt her request was being granted, so she agreed to be helped to a safe location. Meanwhile, Calvin's curiosity was drawn towards the eight-year-old daughter. She was her mother's staunch ally and refused to budge an inch until her mother gave her permission to open the door of the toilet to let the negotiator in. She showed real concern for her mother's safety and well-being. Her demeanour displayed a maturity well beyond her years.

Her mother had been filing for petition with respect to the same cause at various places in her home country for ten years. She demanded that someone in authority review her case with a view to overturn the original decision. (The nature of her case would not be disclosed.) A few of the photos showed her mother pregnant with her during the petitions. Her mother had brought her along to all the petitions since the time she was in her mother's womb.

The girl's calm demeanour was in stark contrast to her mother's earlier wailing and crying. The girl described in chronological order the places that she and her mother had filed the petition. She talked knowledgeably and intelligently.

When Calvin asked about her schooling, the girl had a moment of hesitation. She then discreetly scrolled to the photo album and continued telling him about the petitions, evading the question that had been put to her. All the time, her manners were impeccable.

Before the mother was taken to the ambulance, Calvin took a moment to talk to her. 'Your daughter loves and cares for you very much. She is very obedient towards you. She showed me the photo album. You bring her along to the petitions. I respect your right and determination to fight for justice. But think: What kind of childhood have you given her? She is very mature, well beyond her years—and smart too. She has great potential. Her future and welfare are in your hands. I hope you will bear that in mind. You have a responsibility to give her a decent education. As for now, I shall tell the reporters about your case as you requested. It is up to them how and what they will mention in their papers. I hope you will not contemplate doing self-harm to yourself again. What if an accident occurred? Your daughter is so young. Who will take care of her if something unfortunate happened to you? Take good care of yourself and your daughter.'

The woman looked away, her eyes seemingly peering into the future. As she boarded the ambulance, she turned to look at Calvin. Her face was expressionless. Calvin could not discern what was circulating in her mind. He hoped that the woman would think over what he had said to her at a later time. The eight-year-old daughter smiled and waved goodbye to Calvin.

Calvin's reflection

Occasionally, police negotiators have to handle crises involving people not living in Hong Kong. They may allege that they cannot find justice or a satisfactory solution to some dispute with people in authority. They may also face a crisis due to the inability to cope with some personal problems. They then travel to Hong Kong and create a public scene to attract the media's attention. In some scenarios, they engage in self-harm or threaten to harm themselves.

It doesn't matter whether the person in distress is a Hong Kong citizen or otherwise; a police negotiator provides the same care and service. Even if the person may not necessarily wish to commit suicide but is engaged only in some act of self-harm to fulfil a certain purpose, a police negotiator takes a cautious approach and will not underestimate the chance of an actual suicide attempt. No matter what the circumstance, the assumption is that the person is intent on self-harm, and thus the aim of the negotiator is the same: to persuade that person to abort the attempt.

While dealing with the woman, Calvin's curiosity was aroused by the actions and demeanour of her daughter. The girl was fiercely protective of her mother and proud of being her mom's staunch ally in those petition trips. Calvin could not help thinking whether the girl would still behave the same way when she entered her teens. Her childhood was petition after petition. What about her school life or playing with schoolmates? His advice to the mother might fall on deaf ears, but at least he tried to remind the mother of her responsibility to nurture her daughter and allow her to have a childhood.

Care

A police negotiator's work transcends racial, national, and social boundaries. The woman was not a Hong Kong citizen, and the assistance offered to her was limited at best. The negotiator did his best to explain the situation to the woman. Moreover, he went out of his way to advise the mother to be mindful of her daughter's welfare and upbringing. This scenario is a fine example of showing care.

Chapter Twenty-Eight

A Hong Kong Dream (Attempted Suicide)

Crisis negotiator Sindy Chan

To some mainland women, obtaining residence in Hong Kong and getting a Hong Kong identity card is their dream. Achieving this through marriage is one of the channels. However, it is not easy to face the culture shock and discrimination which is sometimes levelled against them.

From the day that a young mainland wife arrived in Hong Kong to live with her Hong Kong husband, her in-laws looked down upon her and criticised her living habits. They thought that her only and true motivation was to become a recipient of a Hong Kong identity card.

Stigmatised and humiliated, she attempted to take her own life. A police negotiator's sincere and empathetic listening awoke within the woman the reality of what she was doing.

On a summer day in 2011, the police received a report that a young lady in her twenties was standing on a ledge on the outer wall of a public housing building in Sau Mau Ping, Kowloon. The police requested that the Police Negotiation Cadre (PNC) attend the scene to defuse the crisis.

Around two thirty in the afternoon, Sindy Chan and one other PNC member were the first to arrive at the scene. Sindy joined the PNC in 2001. She was an inspector of police at the time of handling this incident. Whilst waiting for a lift at the lobby, the two PNC members exchanged looks of concern as they heard the wailing from the lady more than twenty floors above them.

The flat was at a far end of the building. The fire services had laid a rescue cushion on the ground. However, the positioning of the rescue cushion was restricted by lack of available space. Certainly, it was not in the optimum position, and there was a high chance that it would not be able to break the woman's fall. The woman's emotional state was so unstable that it was too risky to conduct a high-angle rescue at that point in time. Negotiation was the only option.

Sindy walked into a bedroom and stood by the window. What she saw was very disturbing. The woman was standing on a ledge, making no attempt to hold onto anything to help maintain her balance. She was very thin and petite for someone who had given birth just over a month ago.

The negotiator called out to her gently. The woman turned her head slightly towards the direction of the voice, as if in slow motion. She looked but did not seem to see anything. There was a haunting hollowness in her eyes.

Then the woman began to wail loudly. After a period of time, the wailing ceased, replaced by soft shrieks and then muffled sobbing. All this was followed by silence. She gave the appearance of being in a trance.

'I can see that you are in great distress. I am here with you. You are not alone. I am listening to you,' Sindy responded. There was empathy in her voice. By repeating these words several times, she was giving the woman a chance to comprehend and absorb what she was saying.

The woman cried anew with ferocious force. Then she stopped and fell silent once more. She stared blankly into the void.

A picture of a public housing building taken from the ground floor. The ledges on the outer wall are similar to the one mentioned in this scenario.

'I can see that you are feeling very unhappy. I am here listening to you. You are not alone.' The woman was hysterical and in no state to think rationally. To press upon the woman's mind that she had a sympathetic companion and a person willing to listen to her, Sindy repeated the simple but crucial message again and again.

The woman's parents-in-law and husband were not at the flat when the incident occurred. Shortly after, they returned, and the police informed them about what had happened. The PNC support team arranged for them to stay in the adjacent bedroom of the flat. They were instructed not to talk to the woman.

The young couple's one-month-old baby was sleeping in a cot in the living room.

According to the husband, he came to know his mainland wife when he was working in Shenzhen, China. They fell in love and were married. He persuaded his wife to settle in Hong Kong to have a better quality of life. With no money to buy or rent a flat of their own, they lived with his parents in a two-bedroom public housing flat of around three hundred square feet. The flat was originally designed for three persons only, the parents and their son. With the arrival of two new members, living conditions became very cramped.

The husband travelled frequently to the mainland for work. He was aware of the tense relationship between his wife and his parents. His wife urged him to move out. He told her he would consider. In actual fact, he could not afford the high rent of private flats.

The mother-in-law hardly said anything positive about her daughter-in-law. She made such claims as, 'I don't understand why my son married this mainland woman. Ever since she moved in, there has been no peace. I have tried to teach her how we Hong Kong people do things. I don't know whether she is stubborn or stupid. She insists on doing things her own way. When my granddaughter was born, she had no clue about how to take care of her. So unhygienic.'

As the PNC supporter passed this information on to the negotiator, Sindy pictured what sort of life the poor woman had to endure day in and day out. In time, the negotiator's skill in the practice of active listening soothed the woman. She began to share some details about herself.

'We were so happy when we lived in Shenzhen. Then, my husband said we should move. He told me so many good things about Hong Kong. He says it is good for our child's education.

My Hong Kong dream, I believed him. Look where I have ended up now, a public housing flat so tiny, like a bird's cage. My parents-in-law think that I married him to get a Hong Kong identity card. They think I'm not good enough for their darling son. I try so hard to fit in. Do you know what I get in return? My mother-in-law just complains and moans all the time, non-stop. I try to shut out her face, but I can't shut out her voice! The bedroom door is useless. Everything I do about the baby is not good enough. My husband works in Shenzhen and only comes back on weekends, leaving me all alone with them. God knows if he might be dating someone up there. My papa and mama are so far away. I hardly know anyone here. This is like living in hell!' In between these revelations, she would burst out crying. Then she would stop and stand as if transfixed. Her gaze became more and more downcast. She was seemingly ready to jump.

'Hey! Come back! Come back!' Sindy raised her voice to call the woman back to reality.

It was well over an hour. The woman heard her baby's cry and said, 'My baby is crying. Tell my mother-in-law to feed the baby.'

Sindy instinctively felt that the baby mattered the most to her. 'You said your mother-in-law doesn't know how to take care of the baby. You are her mother. You are the most appropriate person to take care of your baby. No one can replace your role. Your baby needs you.'

'Can you feed the baby for me?' the woman pleaded.

Upon hearing this, Sindy deliberately acted as though she had no knowledge about feeding an infant. She wished to reinforce in the woman's mind that the baby needed her care. She posed questions to the woman. 'I don't know what to do. The infant formula—how much is a portion? The bottle over there—is it ready to use? Do I put water or milk powder into the bottle first? Where do I get the water? What's the suitable temperature?' The stream of questioning led the woman back to the real world: she had a baby to look after.

At the same time, the PNC support team talked to the husband about his wife's difficulties and her wish to move out. They could sense that the husband could not move out with his wife in the foreseeable future. Their problems would not disappear overnight. They strove to make the husband fully aware of his wife's dire situation and the importance of showing support and care to her.

The negotiator related her husband's care and great concern for her. There was a gradual change in the woman's countenance. She said, 'I married him not for his money, and not to gain residence in Hong Kong. Even if I have to live in a subdivided flat, I don't mind. At least I have freedom.' In the adjacent room, the husband heard his wife's words.

There was a brief moment of silence. Suddenly the woman changed her posture. From a standing position, she squatted down. Such an unexpected move startled Sindy. *Oh, my God, she's getting ready to jump!* shot through Sindy's mind.

The woman squatted down and started crying anew. This time, however, she wept softly. She was releasing her last bout of sorrow. Sindy knew that it was time to start the rescue. 'Miss, I would like you to stay where you are. Put your hand on the window frame for support. The firemen will help you to come in. There is no need for you to move. No need to hurry. One step at a time. You are doing very well.' She spoke gently to the woman and ensured that she remained alert and calm.

One fireman abseiled down from an upper floor to secure the woman with a harness. Another fireman removed a window frame in the bedroom to climb outside and help her come in.

When the woman was brought back into the flat, she was placed on a stretcher to be taken to the hospital. 'Feed the baby', the woman said, intending her words to be heard by her in-laws and her husband. Sindy spoke to her again to reinforce the hook, that her role as the baby's most important caretaker could not be replaced by anyone. The PNC team also earnestly advised the husband to seek counselling service for his wife from the social welfare department.

Sindy's reflection

Cross-border marriages between people in Hong Kong and China are increasingly common, especially after Hong Kong returned to Chinese rule after 1997. In the eyes of many mainlanders, Hong Kong is modern cosmopolitan and offers more opportunities. Some mainland women may see marriage to a Hong Kong citizen as a gateway to gain residence here. It is their Hong Kong dream. However, Chinese immigrants, especially the low-income groups, may have a hard time integrating into the society due to culture shock and discrimination which is sometimes levelled against them. Some news reports portray these new immigrants to be of low intelligence and uncultured. Consequently, they are being looked upon as second-class citizens. The woman in this scenario lived an isolated life with no social support. Not only did she have to face all that, but she was probably suffering some degree of depression after giving birth to her baby.

The PNC team implored on the husband that he must seek the help of social workers to provide counselling and social support to his mainland wife. When the woman had a chance to know other mainland women in similar situations, she would feel less alone and could learn coping strategies from other people's experiences. Her husband would also benefit from the counselling on how to improve their marital relationship and mediate his parents' discrimination towards his wife.

Care

The woman was hysterical, a state of mind brought on by her abject despair. The negotiator engaged her in active listening and let time be her best friend. Sindy's soothing voice and display of empathy eventually calmed down the woman. The negotiator stressed the mother's unique and irreplaceable role in the care and upbringing of her own baby. The negotiator's care for the woman and the woman's care for her baby resolved the crisis.

A painting, 'Blue', by Karma Castilho.

It's not the end of the world to have failed one assignment. Reflect on the incident and move on. Karma rationalised with herself at the time. She thought she was fine. Nevertheless, she picked up some kitchen tissue paper and started dotting different shades and hues of blue with just a little green on the canvas. She did it with little conscious control of design. When a visual image of a blue and gloomy forest appeared before her eyes, she thought, *What a waste of time.* She tried to erase the painting with a sponge.

In doing this, somehow, in the lower right corner of the painting, the effect turned out to look like a pond in the bush. *Alas! I have sunk to the bottom of the pond!* Her sudden recognition of her disappointment over her failure on the assignment acted as a catalyst for the release of creative energy. From there, she consciously paved out a path. She added sunlight to illuminate a passage leading to somewhere, opening up to her further opportunity for expansive thought and expression.

Police negotiators need to be less judgemental of themselves. They need to accept their own humanity and the fact that they are not and were never meant to be infallible. They need time and space for introspection. If things are troubling them, then it's OK—indeed, admirable—to say that things are not all OK. Acceptance of self, warts and all, is a means of empowerment.

Part H:

THE SEVENTH C— COMMITMENT

Chapter Twenty-Nine

Redemption (Suicide)

Crisis negotiator Ken Fung (Kuen)

Before

I worked in the emergency unit, Kowloon West Region [EU KW], a few years back. I take pride in having made a few dramatic rescues. I use sweet talk, distraction, trick—whatever. It is a battle of wits. If I can get the person to safety, I win. It is all that counts. My peers all say I'm an artful talker.

In a crisis situation, the adrenaline rush pushes one to think and respond quickly. At the same time, the spotlight is on me. The pressure is tremendous. I have gained invaluable experiences. My bosses compliment me on the excellent jobs I have done.

Compliments are good motivation to do better. I am no different. The halo of glory is a pleasant feeling too.

This was Ken Fung's state of mind before he joined the Police Negotiation Cadre (PNC). He applied to join the PNC and completed his training in 2015.

After

In 2017, Ken, in his capacity as a police negotiator, handled an incident of attempted suicide involving an elderly woman. During the course of negotiation, the woman fell many floors and died before his eyes. The incident compelled him to confront an anger so deep that he almost lost control. It is a journey of choking rage, humble introspection, and enlightenment. It is his pilgrimage to redemption.

******

On an evening in 2017, the police received a 999 report that an elderly woman in her late seventies was sitting on a downward sloping ledge on the outer wall of a public housing building in Kowloon, many floors up. To maintain her balance, she was holding on to a horizontal rod attached to the outer wall behind her back for support. The woman resided alone in a flat in that building. She had apparently climbed through the window to sit there.

A picture depicting a sloping ledge on the outer wall of a public housing building. Its appearance is similar to this scenario.

A close-up picture of a sloping ledge on the outer wall of
a public housing building. The arrow indicates how the
old woman might have climbed out through the window
of her flat to sit on the ledge. She could only reach back
one hand to hold on to a horizontal rod for support.

The police requested the attendance of the Police Negotiation
Cadre (PNC). The tactical team, the emergency unit of EU KW,
was already proceeding to the scene. As a sergeant, Ken was
the supervisor of the crew.

Ken's secondary duty was a police negotiator. Ken's supervisor
instructed him to handle the crisis first whilst the on-call PNC
team was on its way.

Upon arrival at the lobby of the building, Ken asked a security
guard at the lift lobby for any useful information regarding the
woman.

'Earlier on, that old woman called the management office here
and asked me to call the police for her. I thought that if she was
able to call and talk to me, she could call the police herself. Thus,
I asked her why she wanted me to make such a call for her, but

she hung up. I did not have time to ask her for more details,' the guard replied.

This information is a good sign. The woman may just be wishing some attention and company, Ken thought.

The doors where the old woman resided were locked. The uniformed police officers entered a neighbour's flat. From there, they could see where the old woman was. The neighbour's flat was at a ninety–degrees angle to the old woman's flat. The lights in the woman's living room remained switched on. The police could thus observe her condition.

When Ken arrived at the neighbour's flat, a female police constable was already talking to the woman. The woman's husband had passed away a few years ago. She was not suffering from any major illness. She was not happy that her relatives had not contacted her for quite some time. Apparently, she felt lonely and depressed.

Ken thought, *the information indicates that she has no immediate, compelling reason to kill herself. This should be a simple scenario and not too difficult to handle. I need to persuade the old lady to let me into her flat and talk to her at a closer distance.*

Ken took over the female police constable's role. There was some distance between him and the old woman. He had to raise his voice almost to the level of a shout to be heard by the old woman.

After a brief introduction, he proceeded to ask her, 'Po Po, I can feel that you are very upset. Can you tell me what made you so unhappy?'

'Little brother, I feel very unhappy. That's why I am sitting here,' the woman replied softly.

'The position you are sitting is very dangerous. Would you like to come back into the flat?'

'No, I won't go in,' the woman replied stubbornly.

'I really wish to know what made you feel so unhappy. But we are too far apart. Here, I need to shout, and I can't hear you very clearly. Can you open your door and let me in so we can talk?'

'I won't open the door for you. You will have to make your own way in!'

'Your doors are locked. Can I ask the firemen to break your doors?'

'Um, yes, okay.'

Meanwhile, an inspector from the fire services informed the negotiator that the woman's relatives had arrived. He thought that they might prove useful in resolving the situation. The relatives seemed quite confident that they could persuade the woman to go back into the flat.

'Inspector, I understand that everyone here wants to rescue Po Po. You mean well to make this suggestion to me. Firstly, we know that Po Po is sitting there, apparently because the relatives have not contacted her for some time. Many possible scenarios might occur. For instance, Po Po and her relatives might have some unresolved disputes. The relatives' unguarded words might be the trigger to make her carry out her threat. A split second is all it takes for her to release the grip. I am in uniform because I am on duty working in this tactical team that is responding to this incident. But I am also a trained police negotiator. The PNC on-call team is on its way. Please trust my professional judgement.' Ken responded. After careful consideration, Ken declined the request of the relatives to speak to the old lady.

'Po Po, the firemen have arrived outside your flat. They will break down your doors now. Do not be alarmed by the noise,' Ken said.

'Little brother, come on in. I'm tired. I'm waiting,' the woman spoke softly. Shortly, Ken heard the sound of a door being opened by force. He saw a fireman enter the woman's flat. Next, he saw the woman turn her head back towards the source of the noise. Then she turned to look ahead. She bent forward and let her body fall. There was a perceptible sound as she hit the ground. People on the ground screamed. She did not survive.

The fire services inspector was standing next to Ken and also witnessed the fall. Ken, despite himself, was filled with a rage. He felt the urge to grab the fireman's arm and shout at him. 'What have you done, man?' However, somehow he managed to quell this urge to vent his outrage on the fireman.

What stopped him? Perhaps it was because Ken could see that the fireman was on the brink of shedding tears. Before becoming a negotiator, Ken would definitely have said those harsh words and laid his hands on the fireman.

In his role as a negotiator, Ken had developed and refined his sense of humanity. It is this very humanity which is quintessential in the emotional heart of the negotiator. By the time Ken reached across to the fireman, this humanity had quelled his anger. His clenched fist and rigid arm was transformed into a caring pat on the fireman's shoulder. He empathised with the fireman and comforted him. 'You did not want such a thing to happen. I know that. I understand your feelings.'

A brief moment of silence passed. He and the fireman prepared to leave the neighbour's flat. The tenant said, 'Fireman brother, thank you very much for your effort. Rotten policeman, no bloody use at all!' The piercing remark stunned Ken. Not every person is friendly towards the police; he knew that. But hearing such hostility under such circumstances ... Standing upright and steeling his eyes directly ahead of him, Ken walked straight past the tenant and out of the flat. The old woman's relatives were at the door of her flat, wailing and crying. They hurled insults at the police, blaming them for not bringing the situation to a successful resolution.

Ken's reflection

In the next two to three days, Ken talked about the incident whenever he met his PNC teammates. Why did the fireman enter the old woman's flat at that point? Why did Po Po decide to let go at that point? Why did Po Po's relatives hurl insults at the police? He was so hurt and angry upon hearing the harsh remarks from the tenant who had allowed the police and firemen to stay in his/her flat to talk to Po Po. He had all these unsolved questions in his mind.

He was both angry and melancholic. His mind was flooded with negative thoughts and emotions. *How come things I see are so grey? I don't feel the usual warmth and cosiness when I come home. What is the matter with me?* These thoughts would not leave him, no matter how welcoming and caring his family members were or how supportive his colleagues were. Only those who have truly suffered from depression can understand the vice-like grip that this negativity exercised over his psyche.

His PNC team members implored him to seek counselling from the police clinical psychologist. They noticed that he was deeply troubled. *I cannot carry on like this*, an inner voice spoke to Ken. On the third day, he decided to sit down and write about the incident. He would then reflect on those issues that he had expressed in his writing.

The woman's background displayed no history of trauma. Again, she had asked the security guard to call the police for her. She might simply be hoping for some attention and company.

However, nothing could be certain at that stage. Perhaps he was too confident about resolving the crisis.

An important lesson he learned was to never underestimate the power of a person's wish to commit suicide. The reason may be trivial, or there may be no compelling motive at all. That does not mean the person will not carry out the act. It only takes one second for the person to decide or change his/her mind. Besides, symptoms of depression are difficult to detect within such a short period.

Why was I so angry at the fireman, who entered the woman's home? Ken thought hard on this question, and his answer came as a revelation.

His original plan was that once the firemen broke the doors, he would leave the tenant's flat and enter Po Po's flat to talk to her. Ken wanted to maintain communication with the woman whilst the firemen were breaking the doors. However, he could not enter the flat at the same time as the firemen. From the fire services' perspective, once they broke the doors, they had to conduct a reconnaissance and immediately coordinate the rescue operation. The tactical part of the rescue necessarily involved the firemen. They would need to secure the old woman with a harness and bring her back to safety, step by step.

No one had expected the old woman to jump at that point. Ken had continued to reassure the woman with respect to what was going on. What made her decide to let go? If he had had the time to continue talking to the woman after the fireman broke the doors, would she change her mind or would she have jumped anyway? The woman was quite tired already. How much longer could she hang on like that? Ken realised there were no answer to these questions.

In the past, firemen had often made high-angle rescues. In some cases, the subject was pulled to safety. There were occasions that the person jumped when the firemen approached. In every case as in this case, the firemen and the police had the same goal in mind: to save a life.

Ken had initially been optimistic about the prospect of a successful outcome to the negotiation. When the expected did not happen, that devastating sense of loss morphed into wrath. Subconsciously, he allowed that wrath to be fixated on an imagined source of blame: the fireman.

I cannot carry on like this, he heard a tiny voice say in his head again. The humanity within him was beginning to manifest itself in his psyche. He took heed of the signal. He took time to communicate and connect with his inner voice. The harsh fact was that nobody knew or would ever know the old woman's state of mind. The harsh reality is that the woman made her own choice to jump and end her life.

Ken looked out of the window and saw the glittering skyline. He was overcome with sadness, but he had made peace with himself. He began to take stock of the lessons that he could learn from this incident—lessons that he could pass on to others.

In the future, he knew that he would be called out to handle a crisis in his capacity as a police negotiator whilst on duty. While he was on duty, he would be wearing his uniform. He would now be mindful of exploring the option of changing into civilian clothes. A negotiator in civilian clothes is less formal and may therefore project a less intimidating image to a distressed person.

In this scenario, the female police constable was already talking to the old woman. In the future, he would consider the option of letting the constable carry on and he would guide her, on how to engage the old woman. Ken could step back and handle other matters; for instance, he could screen what, when, and how much information was to be fed to the police constable.

He could also liaise with the fire services in the coordination of the rescue operation.

As the PNC would call it, this 'fallen case' (as opposed to calling it an unsuccessful case) was particularly affecting because it occurred early in his career with the PNC. This setback affected Ken profoundly, and it was only through introspection and the passage of time that he was able to overcome despair and set his feet firmly on the path to redemption.

Commitment

It was passion and commitment that caused Ken to be so over-come with grief and anger when the woman chose to end her own life. It was passion and commitment that prevented Ken from succumbing to the bouts of anger that threatened to compound his misery. It was the same noble feeling that gave him the courage to acknowledge his inner demons and adopt strategies to control and eventually dispel them. He was able to transform this painful experience into positive lessons. He had the PNC's core values at heart: passion, nobility, and commitment.

Chapter Thirty

The Psychotic Marionette (Suicide)

Crisis negotiator Natalie Lam

How much harm can psychotropic drug abuse do to a person?

A man 'commands' his body to climb on the outer wall of a high-rise building. His mind fails to warn him about the danger or give him any signal to stop. His befuddled mind erodes his physical strength. Exhaustion consumes him. He loses his grip. He survives the fall. Would you say he is lucky?

A drug addict under the influence of a psychotropic drug can become so enmeshed in a fantasy world that the person loses touch with reality. His/her altered mind deceives him/her into enlisting his/her hearing, his/her vision, and virtually his/her whole being into the performance of actions, which can only be described as bizarre. He becomes a marionette under the manipulation of a possessed master. Unfortunately, he himself is that possessed master. Not everyone is lucky enough to wake up in time. No one can tread such a path and come out unscathed.

On an afternoon in 2011, the police received a report that a young man in his early twenties was climbing on the outer wall of a public housing estate in Wong Tai Sin, Kowloon. The police requested that the Police Negotiation Cadre (PNC) attend the scene.

Natalie Lam joined the PNC in 2011. She was a sergeant at the time of handling the incident. Upon arrival on the ground floor, Natalie saw a tiny human figure standing on a ledge on the outer wall of the building, over twenty storeys above the ground. His hands were grabbing on to some support. An image of spiderman shot through her mind.

The uniformed police officers had gathered some information about the man. He was a drug addict and had probably taken quite a high dosage of methamphetamine. Consequently, he was in a state of delirium. Methamphetamine is a psychotropic drug that can wreak havoc in the brain, causing paranoia or hallucinations if taken in high dosages. People who abuse this type of illegal drug can become easily addicted to it.

When Natalie and her PNC team members reached the twentieth floor, a uniformed police officer met them and said, 'The man has moved and is climbing down.' They ran up and down the stairs on foot as the man climbed up and down on the outer wall. They managed to observe his movements through a window in the corridor. The glass pane of the window was very narrow and could not be opened. It thus offered limited vision.

They called to him by his name. 'Hey! Look this way! What you are doing is very dangerous! Do you know where you are now? Hey! Where are you going?' The man started to climb down again and did not respond.

The man's erratic movement made it practically impossible for the PNC team to find a spot to establish contact with him. The fire services had laid out a rescue cushion on the ground. But the cushion could not be moved to follow the man's steps once it was inflated to full size.

'Hey! Man, stop moving!' one of the PNC members shouted again. The man jerked his head towards the direction of the voice. Natalie saw the man's eyes. which were glassy and hollow. It was clear that he was all but oblivious to the danger in which he had put himself.

The man continued to move towards an area where there was a podium on the ground floor. He then stopped on the fourth floor. The crisis negotiators shouted out loud using simple words telling him to stay still.

All of a sudden, the man's hands slipped, and he fell from the fourth floor. Natalie saw the man fall. The limited vision, which she had from the narrow window pane, did not allow her to see where he landed. She heard a distinct sound as the man hit the ground on the first-floor podium.

Immediately, all the PNC team members gathered together to check on everybody's emotional well-being. 'The guy is so young. I feel so sorry for him! I wish so much that I could have talked to him,' Natalie said with a sigh.

'The guy was very high on drugs. He was detached from reality. We have tried our best to help him. Do not be too upset.' The PNC team leader comforted everyone and made arrangements to leave the scene.

The PNC team members were to learn later that the man survived the fall, although he broke both his legs.

Natalie's reflection

Natalie felt powerless in such a situation. The man's delirium made it impossible to establish any communication with him. It was a small consolation that she and her PNC teammates had not interacted with the man on a more personal level. The sadness was therefore not too overwhelming.

Commitment

The man was high on drugs and moved around constantly, making it almost impossible to initiate a meaningful dialogue with him. The PNC team did not give up and persevered in their efforts. They tried every means to find an opportunity to initiate a process of negotiation with the man, hoping that he might respond to them. They were committed to do their best in order to save the man's life.

Chapter Thirty-One

Dicing with Death, a Gambler's Death (Attempted Suicide)

Crisis negotiator Ricky Tsang

A man is heavily in debt as a result of compulsive gambling, and he threatens to commit suicide. He makes a request to see his wife. He wants to ask his wife to repay his debts again. After he is saved, he is granted his wish. What then?

On an evening in 2016, a man in his fifties was sitting on a horizontal drainage pipe on the outer wall of a public housing building many floors above the ground level in Kowloon. The common corridors of these buildings are not enclosed. The concrete wall reached up to half the height of an adult person. Apparently, the man had climbed over the low wall and moved towards the drainage pipe.

A picture of the public housing building depicted in this
scenario. The circle indicates the location of the horizontal
pipe. It was taken in 2018 during the writing of this book.

The police requested the attendance of the Police Negotiation
Cadre (PNC) to defuse the crisis. Ricky Tsang joined the PNC
in 2015. He was a station sergeant at the time of handling the
incident. He and his PNC team arrived at the scene. Ricky took
over as the negotiator. He positioned himself two to three metres away from the man. The man had leaned a bit backwards
so his back rested against the wall.

A close-up view of the horizontal drainage pipe of the public housing building in this scenario. The arrow indicates how the man might have climbed over the low wall and sat on the drainage pipe. It was taken in 2018 during the writing of this book.

The man's appearance was quite striking. He was dishevelled, with an untidy stubble beard. His eyes were bloodshot. Ricky wondered when the man had last slept.

Ricky opened a dialogue. The man said he was married with a son and a daughter. His daughter was studying at a university. His wife and children did not live with him. He had tea with his children sometimes. With some hesitation, he indicated that he was in debt.

'Eh, that afternoon when I woke up, I felt luck was on my side. I really had that good feeling. It was a golden opportunity to win big money,' the man said.

'I see. You feel you have a golden opportunity to win money. You say that afternoon—do you mean yesterday?' Ricky responded in a neutral tone. The man felt encouraged to talk on.

'No, no, not yesterday. I mean three days before. Anyway, I took an evening ferry to Macau. Money can grow more money; you know what I mean? I arrived at the casino, the one where I won a lot of money once. But then ... well, that was a long time ago. ... This time would be different. I just had this gut feeling in me.'

'I see. So, you went into a particular casino that you once won a lot of money.' Ricky acknowledged what the man said.

'Yeah, that's right. I did not have much luck at first. It's normal, you know. Then I made up my mind. I needed to focus on one type of gaming. To win big and win quick, I needed to place a big bet.' From there, the man's eyes sparkled as he plunged boldly into the details of his gambling spree.

Ricky made some remarks to indicate that he was listening. Mentally, however, he was shaking his head. He was in no doubt that the man was addicted to gambling. As he talked, the man looked at Ricky several times, expecting some sort of response, perhaps of censure. Ricky just listened. Feeling at ease, the man continued to talk with considerable animation.

Remaining steadfast to his 'feeling in luck' belief, the man gambled on and on. Winning only increased his craving to win more. Losing made him more determined to reclaim his losses and then get on a winning streak. When he had exhausted the casino chips in his drawer, he was driven to borrow more and more, convinced that a turn in his fortunes was just around the corner.

One day passed, then another. He had no time for sleep. On the third morning, he resolved to sign one last I.O.U. note. He was optimistic that that would do the trick.

'I was aiming for a great game for a finish. I was so close ...' He sighed in anguish. However, there was not a hint of compunction in his voice.

He owed the Macau loan sharks over six hundred thousand Hong Kong dollars (approximately US$76,500) in gambling debts. Two men from the casino escorted him back to Hong Kong and checked out where he lived. He was given a limited time to pay up the debt. He tried to call his wife, but she did not pick up the phone.

On that evening, he could not locate his friend, who resided in this public housing block. With nowhere to go and feeling lonely, he said that he thought about ending his life, so he climbed over the low wall to sit on the drainage pipe.

'My wife had repaid my debts a few times. She always managed to come up with the money in the end! Then we quarrelled. She moved out with the children to I don't know where. Hey, sir, can you help me find my wife? Tell her where I am now, and tell her to come here. I wish to speak with her.'

'What is the reason that you wish to speak with your wife? What do you plan to say to her?' Ricky asked.

'Ah ... you just ask my wife to come here. I will tell her myself.'

The PNC team located the man's wife, who later arrived at the scene. Ricky informed the man that his wife had arrived and they would arrange for him to meet her after he was helped to safety.

'Your wife has arrived already.'

'I don't believe you. Where is she? I can't see her. Tell her to show her face!'

'I am not bluffing. This is her Hong Kong identity card. How could I obtain her identity card if she has not arrived?' They continued talking, but the man was not ready to come back to safety yet.

Midnight arrived. They had been talking for nearly six hours. The daytime temperature was warm. However, a cool breeze picked up, and the temperature dropped. The air was so cool that the negotiators had to borrow blankets from the ambulance men to keep warm. The man was shaking from the cold. His body started to sway sideways. All of a sudden, he jerked his body upright. He was dozing off! The situation was becoming perilous.

The PNC team coordinated with the firemen, who would conduct a high-angle rescue. A team of firemen began abseiling down to reach the man. He noticed the firemen and shouted, 'What are the firemen doing up there? Tell them to stay away. I need to talk to my wife first!'

Ricky said to the man calmly, 'Listen to me. You are very tired and cold. You may fall any time. I am worried about your safety. Everything has been arranged. Once you are brought to safety, we will bring you to meet your wife. You are just one step away from meeting her. Calm down. Let the firemen come to you. You need not panic.' Eventually, the firemen reached him and tied a safety harness around him. He was brought to safety.

His wife was waiting for him inside the ambulance. Ricky accompanied him into the vehicle. The man said, 'Oh, here you are! You will repay the six hundred thousand dollars debt for me, won't you?' That was the man's first remark when he saw his wife. There was no hug, no joy, no sense of gratitude.

The negotiator saw the man's wife lower her head. She did not reply. Ricky advised the man that his gambling habits had alienated him from his family and friends. He advised the couple to seek help from problem-gambling counselling services in Hong Kong. He provided them with the hotline of such an organisation.

Ricky's reflection

Upon listening to the man's talk, Ricky quickly formed the opinion that he was an inveterate gambler. Was he simply using this death threat to coerce his wife into once more paying his debts? Saving him would mean that he would continue to bring problems to his family. Does that fact make the man's life less worth saving? Such a consideration of the value of a person's life is anathema to the ideals held by a negotiator. Ricky and his PNC team held a firm belief that whatever a person's character, it does not make him/her less worth saving. They had the man's interest at heart and were committed to save him.

Commitment

Though critical of the man's gambling addiction, the negotiator's passion and commitment to saving this man's life could not be questioned. To this negotiator—to all negotiators—no life is inconsequential.

Chapter Thirty-Two

Ding! You Are Out! (Attempted Suicide)

Crisis negotiator Arie Chan

Four police negotiators take turns talking to a suicidal man. It often happens this way. What's unusual in this case is that they do not do so by choice. The man assumes a dominant role and rejects the services of one negotiator after the other. Does that mean that the negotiation is not working? What causes the arrogant man to make a complete about-face when he finally aborts the suicide attempt? It is teamwork and commitment.

Arie Chan joined the Police Negotiation Cadre (PNC) in 2004. She handled this incident with three other PNC members many years ago. The different age of these four negotiators was a significant factor in the conduct and resolution of this particular negotiation.

On a late evening, a man in his thirties was seen walking along the edge on a rooftop of a tenement in Shamshuipo, Kowloon. The building was over eight storeys high and did not have a lift. The ledge had no fence and was no more than three feet wide.

The four-member PNC team arrived at the rooftop.

The youngest female negotiator amongst the four started talking to the man. 'Hello, man, I am a police negotiator. I have come here to offer you help.'

'What? You? You are a greenhorn! How old are you? Have you received your adult identity card yet?' The man scoffed and continued walking along the ledge, moving from one end to the other. He talked almost non-stop, and his every sentence inevitably began and ended with expletives. 'Enough, stop! You are disqualified. Ding—you are out! Out of my sight!'

'Hey, wait a moment. Why don't you tell me what had caused you to stand here?'

'Ding! You are out! Go! Go! Go!' the man shouted. The young negotiator withdrew. The dialogue lasted no more than ten minutes.

Arie explained that there used to be a well-known talent contest being broadcast by Television Broadcasts Limited (TVB) on its Chinese television channel, Jade. The TV show was called [殘酷一叮] (Cruel Fate of 'Ding'). If a contestant received a 'ding' from the presiding judge during the performance, that meant that he/she had been eliminated and he/she had to stop singing or performing the minute that the bell was sounded.

Arie was the second negotiator to talk to the man. She was more or less from the same age group as the man. There was no worry about initiating conversation. The man was a chatterbox, but in his conversation with her and all the negotiators, he always included the expletives whenever he spoke.

'Ha, another woman! You look older, more qualified. Come, what's up?'

'Tell me something about yourself. Why are you standing on the ledge? You make me feel uncomfortable the way you stand. Can you come down?' Arie suggested to the man.

'What do you care? Why do you wish to know the life of a scum-bag like me? No job, no money, no love, nothing! You know, that bitch who just gave birth to our daughter ran off with another man. I have no place in her heart anymore! Enough about know-ing me. Hey, let me ask you a question. Do you know whom I respect most?'

At first, Arie tried not to reply directly to the question. She did not wish to let the man control the direction of the conversation because this would probably go nowhere. However, the man started to feel annoyed and said, 'Okay, no more. Ding! Sorry, miss. You are out! Go! Go! Go!' She tried to persist in the con-versation, but the man stood his ground. Their communication lasted for about fifteen minutes.

The third negotiator was a male in his forties, older than the man. Again, the man played the same game. He demanded replies to irrelevant questions and humiliated the negotiator whenever the answers did not match his expectations. He re-mained arrogant, defensive, and controlling. The negotiator managed to engage in conversation with the man for some thirty minutes, but like his predecessors, he was banished by the man.

The fourth and last negotiator came forward. He was in his early fifties and took on the persona of a kindly father figure.

'Young man, we are a four-member team. You have already 'dinged' out three, I am the last one. There is no one else after me. If you 'ding' me out as well, there will be nobody else left to talk to you. Do you really want that?' Silence ensued.

The man was visibly moved by the negotiator's empathic voice. Gradually he became less hostile. He talked about his girlfriend. He hated himself for his failure to achieve success in diverse aspects of his life.

In time, the negotiator felt the man had come to his senses and said, 'You have been talking for so long. You must be thirsty. Let me get you a cup of hot tea. Come.' The negotiator offered a hand to the man.

As the man came down from the ledge, his whole demeanour underwent a complete transformation. This once arrogant and sarcastic young man collapsed into the experienced negotiator's embrace and sobbed fitfully. 'I am so sorry, so sorry. Thank you so much! Thank you, all of you.' The young man muffled these words repeatedly between his loud sobs.

'It's all right, young man. We all go through ups and downs in our lives. You have encountered so many difficulties. It is not easy. You are very brave. You have fallen, but you will stand up again.' The fatherly negotiator patted the man's shoulder as he talked. He comforted him for another fifteen minutes.

Arie's reflection

The scenario was a rather testing one because the man maintained a very hostile persona and wanted to assume charge of the situation. The man played games with the negotiators and dismissed them one by one, claiming that they were lacking in experience. The man had less justification to challenge the negotiators because the next one was older than the former one, suggesting more life experience by virtue of that age.

The negotiators could not help but feel a certain degree of resentment towards the man because of his use of vulgar language and groundless criticisms which he levelled against them. However, they also understood that the man had reached the nadir of despair. By maintaining a controlling stance, he was attempting to persuade himself that he was still empowered as an individual. However, beneath this veneer, he felt utterly worthless. Arie and the other negotiators were professional in their decisions to stay composed and not appear to be confrontational. There was no doubt that the man was touched by the negotiators' sincerity.

Commitment

The suicidal man tried to orchestrate the negotiation. Was this really the case? Probably not; the negotiators simply gave the man the time and space to express and vent all his anger, frustration, and feelings of humiliation. As each negotiator engaged in active listening with the man, she/he collected much useful background information about him that revealed the nature and depth of his problems. In a state of denial, the man casted aside those people who tried to help him. He swore at and demeaned the negotiators one by one. However, the negotiators were consistent in showing him care and concern. They understood that the man had endured a great deal and that beneath his hostile persona, there lay a wounded human being. In the end, the man's persona collapsed, and his anguish was laid bare. Empathy, teamwork, and commitment paid off in the end.

A painting, 'Rainbow', by Karma Castilho.

Karma feels that the experience of gloom and disenchantment are normal and potentially sources of renewal in life. This gloom might well be compared to encountering a rainstorm in some dim corner of a woodland. Somewhere, somehow, the sun's beams work their magic, like a voice in your inner soul reaching out to you. A rainbow appears before your eyes. It is a wondrous sight to behold. You can feel the swirl of vibrant colours cleanse your soul and inject new energy and feelings of self-worthiness and self-belief into your very core. You may not have the opportunity to see a rainbow that often. Bookmark this page as a gentle reminder that each one of us can cultivate our own rainbow. The potential to do so lies within all of us.

Part I:

THE EIGHTH C—
CLOSURE

Chapter Thirty-Three

The Irony of It All (Suicide)

Crisis negotiator Chi-Kwong Wong

How quickly do life's circumstances change! On one particular day, through negotiation, a suicidal person aborts his suicide attempt, and the police negotiator receives a written commendation for his excellent work. On the same day that the negotiator received the commendation, the same man and his girlfriend both jumped to their deaths.

Chi-Kwong 'CK' Wong joined the PNC in 1999. On a summer evening in a certain year, CK was called to attend a scene where a man was threatening suicide. He arrived at an area of squatter huts near Shek Yam Estate, Kwai Chung, south of the New Territories. The squatter huts have since been demolished and replaced by public housing estates.

A man in his early forties lived at one of the huts. The huts were built almost back-to-back, with only narrow alleys for access. The man had climbed onto the rooftop and leaped from one rooftop to another to reach the edge of a hillside. He stood there looking down. One more step forward, and he would fall down a steep hill and perish.

The negotiator had to climb onto a rooftop of a hut to see the man and talk with him. The firemen had tied a harness around him to prevent him from slipping off the slanting rooftop. CK opened a dialogue. The man gradually opened up. He and his girlfriend had been heroin addicts for years. To feed their drug habit, they had committed many crimes and had countless criminal records. They were a disgrace to their families and had no jobs or money. They were destitute. The man believed the only way to end his misery was to end his own life. CK listened with empathy and did not pass any judgement. In time, the man's mood lifted. He listened to the negotiator's advice and came back to safety.

A senior police officer indicated that he would award CK a written commendation, in recognition of his excellent work. CK politely declined the offer and thought no more of the matter.

Several months later, CK read a Chinese newspaper and learnt that the man, whom he had saved, had jumped to his death, together with his girlfriend. *Did I miss something when I talked to the man? What more could I have said to imprint a sense of hope in the man's thinking?* A wave of unspeakable grief consumed his heart while he struggled to find answers to the questions gnawing at him. He subjected himself to a ruthless self-examination. His vision travelled along the walls of his office back down to his in-tray. A single letter addressed to him lay there. The colour of the envelope was a distinctive noble grey, a colour that is reserved for special commendations from senior officers. He knew what it was about. He slid open the envelope and took out a letter that began with, 'Dear Mr Wong, I am writing to compliment you on your professionalism and devotion to duty in successfully handling an attempted suicide incident ... and saving the man's life.' A maelstrom of emotions flooded his consciousness: guilt, grief, anger, and frustration, all equally wounding to his soul.

I did not want the commendation in the first place. I volunteered to become a police negotiator because I genuinely wished to help people who are in crisis situations. It is not a stepping stone to advance my career or a means of receiving written commendations for embellishing my record of service, he thought. At the rather young age of thirty something at that time, he was so full of passion about being a negotiator that he felt he did not need any recognition or compliment of any kind. The sense of being undeserving of praise was made more acute, because he felt he had not done enough to preserve a young man's life and, perhaps indirectly, the life of his girlfriend.

CK's reflection

In time, CK has come to terms with the reality that the couple made their own choice to end their lives. What finally matters is that he did what he could to persuade the man to abort the suicide act at that moment in time. He is not accountable for, and plays no part in, any decision made by people to attempt suicide anew.

Closure

Having saved a life but learning later that the life was lost in the end still caused the negotiator to be overcome with grief. Even though there was a gap of a few months, the negotiator still could not help asking himself whether he had missed doing something at the time of talking to the man. It is never easy to cope with the reality of a fallen case (note: 'fallen' is a term that the PNC uses to describe someone who chooses to end her/his own life in the course of a negotiation).

CK often reflected upon this incident with PNC members in subsequent experience-sharing sessions. He reiterated that there is no failed negotiation. A negotiator should never hesitate to receive a commendation for the good work performed; it is well deserved. Every assignment is an art form that is performed with PNC: passion, nobility, and commitment.

Chapter Thirty-Four

Vanished (Suicide)

Crisis negotiators Natalie Lam, Calvin Cheung, and Steve Li

No amount of professional training or psychological preparation can prepare a police negotiator who witnesses a person falling to his/her death right before his/her eyes. At one point, the negotiator and the person are still engaging in conversation. In a blink of an eye, the negotiator sees the person let go of his/her grip and vanish.

On an afternoon in January 2015, the police received a report that a man in his fifties was standing in a precarious position on the rooftop of an old public housing building in Kowloon. When the uniformed police officers arrived at the roof top, the man was standing outside the metal parapet, which reached half a man's height. His two hands grasped the top horizontal bar of the parapet, he arched his body outward, and his two feet stepped on a strip of horizontal concrete at the bottom of the parapet. He maintained only four contact points to prevent him from falling.

The police requested the attendance of the Police Negotiation Cadre (PNC) to defuse the crisis. Natalie Lam joined the PNC in 2011. She was a sergeant at the time of handling this incident. One male PNC member was talking to the man when Natalie arrived. The man replied in monosyllables to the negotiator's questions. Natalie and some other PNC members were in the background, providing logistics support and monitoring the conversation.

'By midnight, I'll leave. No use talking me out of it,' the man kept repeating. As he talked, he stayed outside the parapet all the time. He moved along and made an L-shape turn round the corner to the other side. At times, he faced the parapet. But without warning, he would release one hand and foot to make a quick half-turn so his face and chest faced outwards. His other leg made it in time to return to the concrete beneath the parapet. In that posture, his legs/toes pointed outwards, and his hands stretched backward behind his back to hold the horizontal bar. Sometimes, he even let go of one hand while in that outward facing position.

A picture of a parapet on the rooftop of a
building, similar to this scenario.

Nearly three hours had passed. The night was bitterly cold. Natalie decided to get some refreshments for her team. She bought drinks and sandwiches. 'Let me have a go,' Natalie told the negotiator and took over the role of talking to the man.

'Hello, how are you? The weather is very cold. You must be tired, standing there for so long. Would you like a hot drink and a sandwich? It's okay to come back in to take a rest, you know.'

The man smiled gently and started talking about himself. He was married with a child. His wife and child resided in China. He visited Hong Kong often for business. Lately, he had lost a lot of money in his business and owed huge gambling debts. He was remorseful about his gambling habit, but he felt it was too late to redress the dire straits in which he found himself.

'I feel very tense when you face outwards with your back against the parapet. I am very concerned for your safety, and I can't see your face. Can you turn back to face me? In this way, we can see each other.' As a result of her gently delivered advice, the man released one hand and leg to make a quick half-turn to turn his body back to face the parapet.

Natalie continued listening to the man. Steve Li, another negotiator, arrived at the scene shortly after 10.00 p.m. He was the team leader of the PNC team that responded to this case and was a superintendent of police at the time of the incident.

Steve discussed with the fire services the chances of bringing the man to safety. The circumstances were not favourable. There was no position for the firemen to set up high angle rescue. They had set up a rescue cushion on the ground, but the man kept moving positions. The chance of him falling onto the cushion was slim.

The negotiators had been talking to the man for nearly six hours. Though he had indeed chosen to make some response to the negotiator's questions, basically he had not wavered at all in his set intention to jump by midnight. He declined to provide contact details of his wife and daughter, who resided in China.

'I'll leave soon. No use trying to persuade me,' he remarked again. Midnight was just a few minutes away. The fire services decided to make an attempt to save the man. They moved towards him slowly.

'I hear what you say. It is not easy for you to tell me about your difficulties. You say your wife and child are in China. You care a lot about them—'

Out of the corner of her eye, Natalie noticed the firemen approaching. She saw the man move his head a fraction, in the direction of the firemen. Without saying a word, the man released his grip and vanished right before her eyes.

Natalie stood, transfixed by the fall. She had wanted to leap forward to catch him, but her whole body froze on that spot. She turned towards her partner, Calvin Cheung, who was behind her. Her mind automatically started counting: *One thousand one, one thousand two, one thousand three* ... Then a thunderous thud assaulted her senses. *It took only three seconds for a person to fall from those storeys to the ground.* Such thoughts filled her mind.

'I hadn't finished talking yet, I hadn't finished talking yet,' Natalie kept saying to Calvin, who came to her side immediately to comfort her. Tears streamed down her face uncontrollably.

Her team helped her leave the building. As soon as Natalie met Steve Li, her PNC team leader, she asked him tearfully, 'Did I say something wrong? Did I miss doing something? I was still talking to him. I hadn't finished.'

Steve comforted her. 'Natalie, you are very shaken. I am deeply sorry for what has happened. Take a few breaths and then listen to me. The man made his choice to end his life. It is not your fault. Not your fault. You have tried your best. You did nothing wrong. It was his choice. You hear me? It was his choice.'

From the time Natalie arrived at the scene to the point that the man let go, about seven hours had expired. She had established a relationship with the man. She had led herself to believe that the situation was hopeful. Her team leader's words calmed her mind and brought her back to reality. *The man saw the fireman approaching. He knew they were there to pull him back to safety. He did not want that,* Natalie mused.

The PNC team learned later that the man landed right next to the rescue cushion and died.

Calvin's immediate concern was the safety of his partner, Natalie. He needed to protect the negotiator and prevent her from endangering her own life, such as trying to rush forward to catch the man.

The man's fall left a vivid imprint on Calvin's memory. As the man loosened his grip and fell downwards, Calvin felt as though the whole world was moving in slow motion. A fireman rushed forward, making a last effort to save the man. Calvin caught a glimpse of the man's eyes looking back at him as he fell. He looked on with the heaviest of hearts as the man vanished from sight.

Afterwards, Steve Li gathered the PNC team together. The PNC team members, especially Natalie, were distraught over the death of the man. Steve and Calvin helped the team members talk about what happened. They became each other's listeners and comforted each other. They reassured each other that they had tried their best.

It was already three in the morning when Natalie arrived home. She had a disturbed sleep and had flashbacks of the incident. The next day, the police clinical psychologist interviewed the PNC team. Natalie talked about her grief. At the same time, she remembered her team leader's words. 'The man made the choice to end his own life.'

Natalie's reflection

The suddenness of the man's fall caught Natalie totally off guard. There was no forewarning because she was still in the midst of a dialogue with the man. Everything had seemed to be going in a positive direction. However, in an instant it was all over. She automatically started the counting when the man vanished from sight. She could not explain her reaction at the time. Perhaps, it was her subconscious, which wanted to erase such a disturbing scene from her memory. She was very disturbed by the image of the man falling. She felt very grateful for the support and care that her PNC teammates offered her.

With the help of the police clinical psychologist, she took time to heal and recover. In time, Natalie overcame that traumatic experience and regained her composure.

Calvin and Steve's reflections

When a person is at a crossroad between choosing life or death, a police negotiator may have a chance to intervene and hopefully help the person find something that matters and hook him/her with that discovery, resulting in that person's decision to choose life over death. Should the person choose death, negotiators go through their own profound journeys, leading to their acceptance of the fact that it was the person herself/himself who made the final decision.

PNC members are like sisters and brothers to each other. This care and support of each other is sincere and constant. The counselling by the readily accessible police clinical psychologist helps the PNC members involved in the incident work their ways through the painful experience. In time, they recover and continue their dedicated mission. They embrace the PNC's motto: 'Who Cares Wins.'

Closure

To learn to accept what had happened in this particular incident, the PNC team gathered to give each other support and comfort. They sought counselling from the police clinical psychologist to put the trauma behind them and reach closure.

Chapter Thirty-Five

To Offer a Second Opinion (Suicide)

Crisis negotiator Rebecca Pang

A police negotiator listens and then offers a second opinion, an option of hope, and a multitude of reasons for the person in crisis to embrace life. That negotiator believes that she/he can persuade that person to choose life over death. In the end, that person may choose to end his/her life. This has to be the most heartrending conclusion that a police negotiator has to face and accept. It is an encounter like no other. It shakes a negotiator's self-esteem and confidence to the core. She/he tortures herself/himself with the question, 'Will the next person I handle choose the same path?'

In the early hours on a day in 2009, the police received a report that a man in his early thirties was seen walking on the top of a narrow awning on the outer wall of an eight-storey tenement in Kowloon. He refused to return to a safe place.

A picture of the tenement depicted in this scenario. The circle indicates the awning on which the man had walked. The negotiator believed the man had climbed to that location from the rooftop. The picture was taken in 2018 during the writing of this book.

Rebecca Pang joined the PNC in 2009. She was an inspector of police at the time of handling the incident. The police provided some background information to her. The man had a fierce argument with his wife at their home. He accused her of having an extramarital affair. In the heat of their quarrel, he stabbed her with a knife. He was also injured in the commotion and ran off. Police subsequently located him at the tenement.

Police officers arrived at the crime scene to find the man's wife gravely injured. The couple had a daughter who was six to seven years old.

The negotiator arrived at the ground floor of the tenement. She entered a flat on the top floor and stood near an opened window. This enabled her to see the man. He was pacing incessantly along the awning from one end to the other. His face betrayed a maelstrom of emotions: agony, anguish, and anger.

A close-up view of the awning depicted in this scenario. A vertical arrow indicates how the man apparently reached the awning by climbing down from the rooftop. Two horizontal arrows indicate how he paced incessantly from one end to the other end. The picture was taken in 2018 during the writing of this book.

The man called himself 'Yakult'. The cotton pad that a uniformed police officer had earlier provided for him to dress his wound was already soaked in blood. The negotiator invited him to come inside the flat so his wound could be attended.

'No, no, I won't come in! Give me a phone. I want to talk to that guy. Let me talk to him. My family is ruined—all because of him!' He went on like that for a while. His tone and words were full of harsh and demeaning epithets.

'OK, OK, how about I hand you a clean dressing?' Rebecca responded. Her PNC team partner passed a clean dressing to her and advised her to put on plastic gloves. She was aware that wearing the gloves was to protect her from possible risk of contamination through coming into contact with the man's blood. Rebecca thought that the formality of wearing gloves might dampen any rapport that had already been established. It would be difficult to re-establish that rapport should it be lost. With this in mind, she wrapped a plastic glove inside her palm, instead of wearing it. In this manner, she gave the clean dressing to the man. She then compressed the blood-soaked cotton with the glove wrapped around it.

The negotiator declined the man's request for a phone to speak with his wife's lover because that would very likely aggravate the situation. She quickly shifted focus to address his request for a cigarette. She secured one from her PNC team and lit it for him. In return, the man agreed to halt his walk along the ledge and remain in one spot, in a position, where they could see each other.

'If something happened to me, would some institution take care of my daughter? I am sorry to have caused you so much trouble. You don't need to stay here. Tell the police officers and the firemen to leave. Let me be.' Such a question and the remarks from the man which followed were cause for alarm. Rebecca implored him to accept the fact that nobody else could replace the love of a father for his daughter.

'How's my wife? Is she still alive? Is she dying?' the man asked.

'As far as I am aware, she is still alive.' Rebecca decided not to elaborate any further. She knew that his wife was still in critical condition after surgery. She was to learn later that his wife pulled through. The man walked back and forth again and gazed downwards a few times. The fire services had placed a rescue cushion on the ground.

'Yakult, come back. You promised to stay in that spot where I can see you. Remember your promise!' Rebecca called out. Yakult walked back with his fingers still holding onto the cigarette. He continued the actions of inhaling and exhaling, but no more smoke came out. The tobacco rod was long burnt out. He turned sideways towards the negotiator. Their eyes met. He said, 'Thank you.' His tone was sincere but imbued with a deep and disturbing sadness.

The negotiator would not let her mind contemplate the unthinkable. She responded earnestly, 'Hey, Yakult, there is no need to thank me. We are all here to help you, and we hope you can come in.' She continued talking to him in that manner. He walked away out of her sight again. It was nearly five in the morning. The sky was still quite dark.

Suddenly, there was a noise. Something dull and heavy had hit the ground. Rebecca's first thought was, *Well, it is very early morning. It must be someone throwing out a big garbage bag.* Worried that the noise might startle the man, she shouted, 'Yakult, do not be alarmed! It's only—' The negotiator did not finish the sentence when she heard a message.

'Landed! Landed!' someone shouted through the police beat radio, which was within her earshot. She stood frozen to the spot. The beat radio traffic continued.

'On the ground or on the rescue cushion?'

'On the ground! On the ground! He dropped right next to a uniformed police officer. Scared the shit out of him. The officer's fine, not physically hurt.'

Rebecca was stunned by what had just transpired. Rebecca's teammates accompanied her downstairs and left the building through the back door, away from the sight of the corpse.

It was early morning already. She and her teammates had a brief period of rest. In the afternoon, they gathered in the office of the police clinical psychologist (PCP) for a debriefing. She was offered the option of seeing the PCP by herself. She felt comfortable talking over the incident with her team members. They each shared their feelings. The PCP invited everyone to talk about the episode and the scenes that were striking or made an impression on them.

Rebecca recalled the man's incessant walking, the way he still sucked at the tip of the cigarette even though the tobacco rod was all burnt out, and the way he looked at her and said thank you. She then realised that he had looked down to choose a point, where he would come to rest—a position not covered by the rescue cushion.

Rebecca's reflection

Rebecca resumed work, and life moved on. In the days that followed, she had repeated flashbacks of the episode. In her quiet moments, she wanted to cry, but the tears wouldn't flow.

She told her mother about the incident. They were very close to each other. It was only later that Rebecca realised that she must had been in a pretty bad state, because her mother was so worried about her.

Closure

The negotiator's experience of flashbacks gradually subsided. For the first few months after the incident, her team was called out to resolve crisis situations. Rebecca was told that it was her choice to decide when she was ready to resume in her role as negotiator. She was truly grateful for the counselling by the police clinical psychologist and the care and support of her team members and colleagues.

In time, Rebecca overcame that period of self-doubt and came out from her cocoon of sadness. She reached closure and regained her composure and self-belief.

Chapter Thirty-Six

It's OK to Say
I Am Not OK (Suicide)

Crisis negotiator Wilbut Chan

A police negotiator talks to a heroin drug trafficker for over eight hours, hoping that he would abort his suicide attempt. The man jumps in the end and takes his own life. The thundering sound of his body striking the ground was such that it would live long in the memories of those who were present at the scene.

On a weekend in a certain year, a man in his late thirties was standing on the edge of a terrace on a high-rise building, many floors above the ground in Tuen Mun, the New Territories. Unable to persuade the man to come down, the police requested that the Police Negotiation Cadre (PNC) attend the scene to assist in the resolution of the crisis.

Wilbut Chan joined the PNC in 1999. He and his PNC team arrived shortly after they were called. Wilbut took up the role of negotiator. He was a chief inspector of police at the time of handling the incident.

The man confessed that he had been a heroin drug trafficker for years. 'I'm a scumbag. I have ruined many people's lives. My hands are filthy. I lost count. Why am I still alive and standing? I don't deserve to continue living. My mom—she is over there, waving at me. She is calling me to join her in the other world, to keep her company.' The man continued talking like that in between long stretch of silence.

Wilbut listened with practised patience and acknowledged the man's predicament. At times, the man looked down or far away. Fearing that the man might be contemplating jumping, Wilbut would say, 'Hey! Come back!' The man then seemed to come back to the present.

'Hey, man, would you like some water?' There was no answer from the man. Wilbut said, 'OK, I just need to go to the wash-room. My partner, this guy next to me here, has been with me all this time. He will take my place for the time being.' They had been talking for over eight hours. As the man declined the offer of water, the negotiator made an excuse to walk away to drink some water and to take a break.

Just before the negotiator turned away, he caught a glimpse of the man's face. He thought that he had seen a human skull. He could not explain what he saw, but that image has been implanted in his memory ever since. Not long after, he heard the man shout, 'Fuck off!' Then he heard a grating sound like a big heavy bag of flour hitting the ground. He turned back. The man was not there anymore. His lifeless body lay on the ground just off the margin of the rescue air cushion.

Wilbut gathered his members, about eight of them, and they comforted each other. Everyone said that she/he was OK. Together, they made their way away from the scene.

A few days later, a team member contacted Wilbut. He was obviously distressed. 'I can't shut off his words. I hear the words "Fuck off" over and over again. And that dull thud of his body striking the ground—it won't leave me alone. Even when I'm talking with people or sleeping, I can't put a stop to it. I have trouble sleeping.' Wilbut contacted other team members, and most of them felt troubled by the experience.

On the same day, Wilbut gathered together his team members who had attended that particular incident. A police clinical psychologist held a number of counselling sessions with the group. She encouraged them to express their feelings to exorcise the demons that were preying on their psyches. Under the guidance of the police clinical psychologist, they regained their composure and self-confidence, and the flashbacks gradually subsided.

Wilbut's reflection

A lot of the time, police officers have tough personas, which they feel that they must maintain in the eyes of their colleagues and the general public. The PNC team members all appeared OK at first. However, after a few days, problems began to emerge. As close and committed colleagues, they were able to speak openly and honestly and use each other as sounding boards. With counselling from the police clinical psychologist, they permitted themselves to step outside their personas and admit that they were only human.

Closure

In this case, the PNC team experienced a traumatic incident. The symptoms did not surface immediately. However, some PNC members required follow-up help. The system and resources necessary for the healing process to be affected were made available to them. They were thus able to achieve closure over time.

Conclusion

A short recap of the thirty-four incidents discussed, using the eight Cs model.

Chapters three to six depicted the initial action of cordon, put in place prior to a negotiation. Police officers set up a cordon in a public area to separate the crowd of bystanders from a man holding a knife (chapter three). Police officers cordoned off the report room where a man was holding a broken piece of glass against his neck. Again, the tactical team formed an inner cordon right behind the negotiator to protect him/her in case of an emergency (chapter four). The tactical team cordoned off the corridor outside a residential flat and then formed an inner cordon behind the negotiator. As a result of their vigilance, they reacted in a timely manner, using their armadillo shields, to prevent the assailant's knife from penetrating the negotiator's forehead (chapter five). Police officers cordoned off a corridor in a police station, where a policeman was threatening to commit suicide with his service revolver (chapter six).

Chapters seven to ten demonstrated the use of command. A man demanded to see his ex-girlfriend and held her mother captive to achieve this end. Having weighed up the factors and circumstances, a police incident commander made a decisive move and pinned the man down (chapter seven). An armed man barricaded himself inside his flat and made minimal response to the negotiation team. The police incident commander considered the information at hand and the way in which the incident might end badly. His/her final decision was to make a forced entry. This was a judgement call (chapter eight). Effective command, control, and coordination resulted in the successful rescue of a suicidal woman at the Ting Kau Bridge (chapter nine) and an old man who intended to jump off a building when the signature tune, which signalled the start of the evening news, was heard (chapter ten).

Chapters eleven to fourteen depicted the power of communication. The PNC team tried to overcome the difficulty of talking to a man, who was behind closed doors, by lowering a negotiation throw-ball from an upper floor into the man's unit; that device had to be retrieved due to the man's hostile reaction to it (chapter eleven). The empathetic listening of three male negotiators had temporarily caused a distraught woman to waver in her determination to take her own life. Then, a female negotiator's caring and simple message finally struck a respondent chord within the woman (chapter twelve).

An old woman misinterpreted her family members' good intentions and thought that they intended to abandon her in a home for the elderly. She might have thrown herself off a high-rise building if not for the communicative skill of the negotiator, which improved the woman's mood (chapter thirteen). The PNC team patiently let time run its course as they engaged in active listening with a man who had barricaded himself inside his premises with a boy. At a timely moment, they talked to the man as a team and encouraged him to surrender (chapter fourteen).

Chapters fifteen to nineteen demonstrated the control of emotion. The tactical team officers became more and more frustrated as a barricaded person maintained a stubborn stance and would not stop his verbal abuse. The negotiator had to manage the tactical team's emotions, as well as his own negative sentiment with respect to the subject (chapter fifteen). Three girls formed a bond and determined to commit suicide together. A negotiator patiently listened to the girls and empathised with the cause of their anger and distress. Her perseverance with active listening gradually gained the girls' trust (chapter sixteen). A negotiator engaged in active listening with a burglar who made four challenging requests (chapter seventeen). A negotiator reminisced with a frustrated, retired police officer. This resulted in the amelioration of his anger, which he had felt due to the fact that he perceived that his family was not supportive of him (chapter eighteen). Dr Vecchi, the negotiator, stayed within a man's frame of reference as he engaged in active listening. Gradually, the man's emotional state became more relaxed, so much so that he became amenable to the employment of a coping strategy (chapter nineteen).

Chapters twenty to twenty-three foregrounded the value of the coordination of intelligence. The PNC support team gathered and attributed meaning to information about the subject person's family background and advised the negotiator, with respect to the direction that the negotiation should take (chapter twenty). The PNC team had obtained a detailed picture based upon the intelligence gleaned from the murderer's wife, his niece, and from neighbours. The communication of this information to the police incident commander enabled him to make an informed and timely decision (chapter twenty-one). A continual flow of information was passed on to the negotiator so he could sustain the negotiation. A seemingly innocuous piece of observation that was passed on to the negotiator turned out to be a key factor in the negotiation process (chapter twenty-two). The successful resolution of a plane hijacking incident in 2000 demonstrated the crucial role played by the coordination of intelligence (chapter twenty-three).

Chapters twenty-four to twenty-eight illustrated the element of care. As he was wheeled away by the ambulance crew after he aborted his suicide attempt, a man held the negotiator's hand to express his appreciation of the way in which this crisis was averted (chapter twenty-four). A man's distressed, emotional state was alleviated by the negotiator's kind words and their appreciation of each other's poetic talents (chapter twenty-five). The negotiator patiently listened to a distraught man. This ultimately led to the realisation on the part of the man that his aged parents' love and care for him was boundless (chapter twenty-six). The negotiator was able to persuade a woman to abort her intention to pursue an act of self-harm. Concerned for the woman's daughter, who had accompanied her mother to many petitions, the negotiator advised the woman to be mindful of her daughter's welfare and upbringing (chapter twenty-seven). The negotiator listened patiently and repeated simple messages of care and companionship to a heartbroken young mother (chapter twenty-eight).

Chapters twenty-nine to thirty-two illustrated commitment. The negotiator felt profound grief and anger when an old woman jumped to her death, because he felt that he should have been able to persuade her to abort the suicide attempt. As a sense of his own humanity led to self-forgiveness, he embraced the core values of a negotiator with a humble but wiser heart (chapter twenty-nine). A drug addict high on psychotropic drugs and an inveterate gambler diced with death in different ways. The negotiators never wavered in their commitment to saving the two persons' lives (chapters thirty and thirty-one). A man hurled insults repeatedly at four negotiators. The negotiators persevered in active listening without losing their tempers. In the end, the man's hostile persona dissipated, and his anguish was laid bare (chapter thirty-two).

Chapters thirty-three to thirty-six dealt with closure. The negotiator received a written commendation for having saved the life of a man who was threatening to kill himself. He then learned that the man he saved made a second attempt and committed suicide with his girlfriend (chapter thirty-three). A man jumped to his death right in front of a negotiator, and a man said thanks to the negotiator, walked out of her sight, and jumped to his death (chapters thirty-four and thirty-five). The PNC members initially indicated that they were OK after experiencing a fallen case. However, several of them had flashbacks a few days after the incident had occurred (chapter thirty-six). The negotiators in all these cases experienced trauma to different degrees and only gradually made peace with their inner emotions.

***

Sometimes we may feel overwhelmed by our personal problems. Some people may reach a point where they feel they are unable to cope with the seemingly never-ending misery and disappointment in life which they are experiencing. Unfortunately, some of these persons may engage in self-harm or even try to kill themselves. Age, gender, upbringing, personal background, and a multitude of other internal and external factors impact, singularly or in combination, a person in crisis, compelling that individual to act in such a way at a particular point or stage in her/his life. Such people in emotional crisis are overwhelmed by tunnel vision, perceiving death to be the only viable alternative to the anguish they are experiencing.

Hong Kong's negotiators are very special, selfless, and altruistic people. Gilbert has said, 'Our best negotiators are passionate people who like to communicate with others from all walks of life.' They hold fast to the notion that every life has value and that life is to be preserved, no matter the personal cost to themselves. The Police Negotiation Cadre is the personification of the principle of the sanctity of life. The aim of our negotiators is to dispel, in part or in whole, that tunnel vision through which distraught people see life. Negotiators are trained with the understanding that people in crisis need to be heard and feel that they are understood. If the negotiators can develop a relationship with distressed individuals, then this can ultimately lead to behavioural change and an end to the crisis. This relationship is constructed through the deployment of five skill sets: active listening, empathy, rapport, trust and influence.

We may well marvel at the selflessness and skill deployment of members of the Police Negotiation Cadre. We may lament the fact that we ourselves do not have the capacity to preserve the lives of people beset by emotional crisis. However, in all truthfulness, each one of us, in our own distinctive way, can address the loneliness and isolation of other people. Every human being has a basic need for recognition and companionship. If these basic needs go unfulfilled, then individuals become vulnerable to debilitating psychological conditions which, if untreated, can quickly degenerate into a mindset where suicide seems to be the only logical course of action. Through simple acts of greeting and recognition, we may well have a positive effect on the mood of an isolated individual and give that person at least some glimmer of hope that there may indeed be a place for him/her in society.

Mother Teresa famously said, 'Maybe in our own family, we have somebody who is feeling lonely, who is feeling sick, who is feeling worried, are we there? Are we willing to give until it hurts in order to be with our family or do we put our interests first? ... We must remember that love begins at home and we must also remember that the future of humanity passes through the family.'

American poetess Emily Dickinson asserted in a poem,

> If I can stop one heart from breaking,
> I shall not live in vain;
> If I can ease one life from aching,
> Or cool one pain,
> Or help one fainting robin
> Unto his nest again,
> I shall not live in vain.

Albert Schweitzer said, 'The purpose of human life is to serve and to show compassion and the will to help others.'

We believe that being human comes with a moral imperative to assist other human beings as they seek to find meaning and happiness in what is a perplexing and often troubling world. We may not possess the skills and moral fortitude of the members of the police negotiation cadre. But we can all greet and recognise our fellow human beings who are obviously lonely and vulnerable, whether they be close friends, family members, or individuals in the wider community.

It is the sincere hope of Connie and Gilbert that this experience sharing may be a source of reference and inspiration for likeminded professionals who are dedicated to the resolution of crisis incidents and the prevention of death by suicide. It is also hoped that the general reader may enjoy reading this book and come to a greater understanding of the nature and extent of loneliness and hopelessness in contemporary urban society. If the reading of this book awakens the compassion which resides in all of us, then we will be richly rewarded for having written this book. And may the selflessness of the members of the Police Negotiation Cadre inspire you to be an agent of social good in whatever way that best utilises your skills and interests in the great pageant of life which is human existence.

Bamboo, by Karma Castilho.

This bamboo woodland symbolises a community. People from all walks of life gather in this agora. The variations and idiosyncrasies that characterise the individuals are represented by a kaleidoscope of colours. They may be people of different race, nationality, cultural, and religious background and affiliation. They embrace and accommodate each other's differences. They support each other's uniqueness and aspirations. The side branches stretch out to connect with other bamboo trunks. Together, they build up strength and resilience against the storm. This is an allegorical representation of the human potential, through empathy and a recognition of the oneness of the human experience, to forge a powerful armour to temper misery and loneliness in the diverse societies of our world.

In summary, this agora of bamboos is an exemplar demonstrating the power of connectivity and mutual support. Everyone in a community can play a part in helping friends or family members around us—indeed, even the strangers we meet in our journeys through life. Being a non-judgemental listener and offering a supporting hand imbues troubled souls with new hope, a way to penetrate the darkness which encircles them, and a way to find their way through the shadows into the light. That is the birthright of every human being.

What we call the beginning is often the end
And to make an end is to make a beginning.
The end is where we start from.

—T.S. Eliot

Courage, by Karma Castilho.

Hope, by Karma Castilho.

Freedom, by Karma Castilho.

Appendices

Interview with Dr Paul Wai Ching Wong D. Psyc (Clinical) on 2 October 2018 by Connie Lee Hamelin

What do you do, and what are your areas of interest?
I am an associate professor at the department of social work and social administration, at the University of Hong Kong. I am a clinical psychologist by training, and one of my research and clinical interests is suicide prevention. I was the national representative of Hong Kong with the International Association of Suicide Prevention between 2010 and 2015.

I am honoured to have been involved in multiple research studies in suicide prevention in Hong Kong since 2003, at which time I was with the Centre for Suicide Research and Prevention at the University of Hong Kong (the Centre). In particular, I was actively involved with one of the very first psychological autopsy studies on completed suicide in this region; co-created several community-based suicide prevention projects with various stakeholders, including the Hong Kong Police (HKP); and initiated a study on helping people bereaved by suicide, in partnership with the Department of Health's Forensic Pathology Unit and associate professor Dr Philip Beh.

How did you become connected with the Police Negotiation Cadre (PNC)?

In 2003, Gilbert, the commanding officer of the PNC, paid a visit to the centre with a group of trainees. At the time, he was delivering training to a group of social work assistants from the Social Welfare Department (SWD). These were people who might need to handle suicide-related issues in the course of their work. The SWD people processed applications for the Comprehensive Social Subsistence Allowance (CSSA). That's how we first became acquainted.

On another occasion, a team from the Carelinks Cadre of the HKP also paid a visit to the centre to learn about our work. The cadre was established in July 2005 under the management of the police psychological services group. Police officers and civilians working in the police force are eligible to join this unit upon passing selection interviews. Their mission is to nourish a caring culture in the workplace and provide care and support to colleagues in need. The founding chairman of the cadre is Gilbert.

I have had frequent contacts with Gilbert since then. Upon his invitation, I gave talks to the PNC members about my work on suicide prevention, from a research perspective. In 2007, when the HKP hosted the International Negotiation Working Group Conference in HK, I was invited to their dinner event (and surely that was a memorable night of my life), and since then, I have been deeply impressed with the hard work performed by negotiators involved in suicide prevention. In 2015, I become an honorary researcher of the Hong Kong Police College as a result of my collaboration with the HKP. This honorary role is a source of great pride on my part.

You and the PNC have collaborated on a research project related to suicide prevention. Can you elaborate upon this?

The PNC in HK does unique suicide prevention work, in comparison with other places in the world. From the latest statistics provided by the centre, almost 50 per cent of suicidal persons in Hong Kong have chosen jumping from tall buildings as their way of ending their lives. Very often, a person standing on a rooftop or on a structure on the outer wall of buildings has a high chance of being seen by members of the public, who will dial 999 to call the police. The chances of police being involved in suicide crisis intervention are far more likely because of this unique socio-environmental context. In a nutshell, the PNC can reach many intensive suicidal cases in HK because suicidal acts are more visible than other places in the world. Hence, I wished at that time to explore with the PNC an understanding of the psychological journey of the aborted suicidal individuals. In other words, the research wished to explore a person's mental turmoil that had driven him/her to seriously contemplate suicide; I wanted to know those mental footprints that led an individual to abort the suicidal intent after intervention by the PNC. I also wished to know about the intent and actions of that individual after the initial suicide crisis was resolved.

In 2011, the highly competitive general research grant managed by the HKSAR government's University Grant Council approved funding for us so we might study this phenomenon. Over seventy members of the PNC assisted in the research. They acted as intermediaries in explaining the study to a would-be suicide person, provided a specifically designed suicide prevention booklet to that person, and invited him/her to participate in subsequent interviews.

From 2012 to 2015, we approached a number of aborted suicide attempters and managed to talk to about ten people who selflessly shared with us their suicidal processes. This study was one of, if not the most, challenging studies in which I have been involved. However, it was very worthwhile to have done it because it allowed us to witness the suicidal processes of ten suicidal individuals in Hong Kong. For readers who are interested to know about the methodology of our study, please visit https://www.researchgate.net/publication/312257723_The Methodology_and_Research_Participation_of_Participants_in_ the_Aborted_Suicide_Attempt_Study.

You have also conducted another research on 'Psychological autopsy of suicides in Hong Kong' and studied hundreds of suicide notes'. Can you elaborate?

Through talking to families of people who have completed suicide, and by studying their last writings, I sincerely believe that 'one suicide is too many'. The pain that the families have to go through for the rest of their lives, the impacts that each suicide could bring to the family, community, and society, and the invisible scars that some people have to carry for years not only have an impact on me but also gives me the motivation to do more in the field of suicide prevention. In particular, from the suicide notes that I have read, I always emphasise that if there was a caring person next to the suicidal person at the time he/she was writing the note, I am very sure that he/she could be persuaded into not choosing death as a solution to his/her (in all likelihood) temporary problem.

What aspects of your academic research may impact upon suicide intervention through negotiation?

Following the above, I sincerely believe that the PNC is doing something that fills the service gaps that our society cannot cover. Hong Kong does not have a lot of mental health professionals, and our suicide crisis intervention provided by non-government organisations is very limited. PNC often acts as the last life-saving rope for the suicidal persons when 'traditional' suicide prevention services are not available.

After having worked with the PNC in the area of suicide prevention for over a decade, what is your impression of the police negotiators?

I can confidently say that the PNC play no small part in saving the lives of the suicidal people whose paths they cross. The unpredictability of turn-out hour and duration of the negotiation episode invariably take a toll on their sleep, family time, and social lives. Not to mention that they still have their principal job to do after finishing the volunteer work. From what I know, it is not uncommon that a PNC team has worked throughout the night, and they have just enough time to go back home for a quick shower before starting the following day's work.

Through my years of interaction with the PNC, I have witnessed their unwavering belief in the intrinsic value of human life. They will do everything in their power to try to save a suicidal person. It is not about physically bringing the person to safety. They are crisis counsellors and de facto 'mind rescuers'. I have a lot of respect for their passion and commitment and their motto, 'Who Cares Wins'.

I think this book is a great platform for readers to understand and appreciate the police negotiators' job. Most important to me, I have learned a lot about suicide prevention from the PNC and through interacting with the suicidal persons and their families. Suicide prevention efforts should not be confined to mental health professionals, psychiatrists, psychologists, the police, and suicide-intervention organisations. Different organisations can work together to share experiences and good practices, in a multidisciplinary approach. Individuals can also play a part. If a friend or family member is in distress, offering to listen and seeking professional help may save a life. I reiterate my belief that one suicide is too many.

PNC is my teacher. Thank you, Gilbert and the negotiators, for giving me the opportunity to learn from all of you.

Interview with Dr Gregory M. Vecchi, PhD, on 7 November 2018 by Connie Lee Hamelin

When and how did you join the Federal Bureau of Investigation (FBI)?

I was a law enforcement officer for twelve years before applying to join the FBI in 1996. I shall mention my previous jobs first in three other federal agencies.

From 1989 to 1992, I worked as a special agent in the US Army, Criminal Investigation Command (CID), in Fort Bliss, El Paso, Texas. I investigated violations of federal law relating to military personnel. I specialised in crimes against persons, white-collar crime, and drug suppression. I also conducted in-depth crime scene investigation and analysis.

From 1992 to 1993, I worked as a special agent in the US Department of Agriculture in Atlanta, Georgia. I conducted investigations into food stamp fraud.

From 1993 to 1996, I worked as a special agent in the US Department of Justice in McAllen, Texas. I worked on corruption investigations involving US immigration employees and border patrol agents, among other things.

I always aspired to join the FBI. On my third attempt, they were looking for people with military and law enforcement background. I met their criteria and was accepted in 1996. I then completed training at the FBI Academy in Quantico, Virginia.

My first job in the FBI was as a special agent in Miami, Florida, where I worked from 1997 to 2003.

How and when did you become a negotiator in FBI?

I was hooked into becoming a negotiator from the beginning. Incidentally, I was leading an investigation involving drugs and organised crime. On a day of a planned operation, I called for a special weapons and tactics (SWAT) team to conduct a raid on a house and arrest a suspect. I recall seeing the FBI van arriving. The door of the van swung open, and a group of young and strong SWAT team guys emerged in full tactical gear. The last person who came out of the van was a middle-aged man who was bald and quite opulent. His laid-back demeanour was in stark contrast to the other SWAT team guys.

After the SWAT team received their briefing and left to prepare for the raid, the older man came up to me and said, 'Tell me about your guy.'

I said, 'What else do you wish to know? I've just told you every-thing there is to know.'

'I'm not interested in that,' he said. 'Tell me what you know about him. What is he like as a person? What does he like or dislike? How about his family? Has he got a wife, girlfriend, kids? Tell me everything that you know about this guy.'

After having worked on my target for three years, I had col-lected a lot of intelligence on his background and private life. I thought, 'Why would he want to know all that?' Because I was a rookie in the FBI, I didn't challenge him and told him everything he wanted to know. As he was about to leave, he turned back and said, 'Just one more thing. Give me his cell phone number.'

I thought, 'Whatever,' and told him.

When the time came to make the arrest, the SWAT team was in position ready to kick in the doors. It was my first big case, and I was quite nervous. The minutes ticked by, and nothing hap-pened. Then all of a sudden, the door of the premises opened, and my target—that notorious and dangerous criminal—walked out with hands open in the air. He surrendered just like that.

I found out very quickly that the fat bald man with whom I was not impressed was a hostage negotiator. I told myself then that I wanted to be like him. That was what launched me on this whole journey.

Is there some kind of selection or training involved in becoming a crisis negotiator?

Yes, there is. If I indicate interest in becoming a crisis negotiator, I first work as an auxiliary negotiator for a trial period. This is a vetting process where other negotiators evaluate my suitability to see whether I possess the qualities of a negotiator. I get to do everything from coaching, doing situation boards, liaison and intelligence analysis, and other related jobs. If I meet their expectations, they will recommend me to attend a certification training at the FBI Academy in Quantico, Virginia. The training is run by the crisis negotiation unit. It is a very tough and demanding two-week training program. I got through it and obtained my official certification as a negotiator. After that, I started working as a FBI crisis negotiator. I did a lot of negotiation work and gained lots of experience.

How did your career progress as a FBI negotiator?

After 2003, I was deployed to the rapid deployment logistics unit of the critical incident response group in Quantico, Virginia. Later, as supervisory special agent, I was deployed to Baghdad, Iraq, to work in the warzone in support of the FBI counterterrorism mission. The work practically involved picking up human remains and evidence from bomb explosions to build up intelligence and identify terrorist attacks being planned for the US mainland. I also worked in the background in coordinating and planning the Saddam Hussein interview and interrogation. I didn't work in negotiation in that assignment. Nevertheless, I negotiated contracts and deals in arranging logistics and getting resources with the skill-sets as a negotiator.

From December 2004 to January 2006, I was supervisory special agent in the crisis negotiation unit of the critical incident response group, Quantico, Virginia. There, they trained people to become negotiators. I travelled around the world to give training and attend conferences. I also coordinated and managed responses to international kidnapping situations by providing operational consultation to local, state, federal, and foreign agencies.

In January 2006, I was assigned as supervisory special agent in the Behavioral Science Unit at the FBI Academy. I became unit chief supervisor special agent in August 2008 and stayed until October 2011.

From October 2011 to February 2014, I requested a transfer to work in Rapid City, South Dakota, because I wished to retire there. I stepped down as a regular agent and no longer took up a supervisory role. I conducted field hostage negotiations and used advanced behavioural techniques in investigating organised crime, Indian country violent crimes, and others.

Upon my retirement in February 2014, I continued to pursue my passion in crisis negotiation and other areas of expertise that I had gained from my FBI career. Two years later, I moved to Missouri to take up a job. Currently, I am an assistant professor in the Department of Criminal Justice, Legal Studies and Social Work at Missouri Western State University. I also work as a reserve deputy sheriff in Buchanan County and Clinton County of the Missouri sheriff's department. These two positions are volunteer positions that allow me to continue being a law enforcement officer and engage in crisis negotiation.

How did the Hong Kong police link up with you in providing negotiation training to the PNC?

I am well-known around the world for the behavioural influence stairway model in negotiation that I developed. Gilbert invited me to come to Hong Kong to train the PNC in the use of that model. I came to know Gilbert in 2010. I shall go back a little bit to talk about my years as unit chief supervisor special agent of the Behavioral Science Unit from 2008 to 2011.

The FBI has run a program called the National Academy since 1935. The purpose of the program is to enhance positive relationships between the FBI and other law enforcement agencies worldwide. It invites, at no cost, the best of the best law enforcement officers (LEA) from around the world to participate in a ten-week program where the officers can take classes in behavioural science, leadership, forensics, and communication at the FBI Academy in Quantico, Virginia. In 2010, Gilbert Wong, a detective superintendent of the HK police at the time, was nominated to participate in the program. There were other LEAs nominated to attend the academy, such as the Metropolitan Police of the United Kingdom, the Australian Federal Police. Gilbert took all four subjects offered by the Behavioral Science Unit.

As chief of the Behavioral Science Unit, I invited Gilbert to take an additional one-week program on beyond survival towards officers' wellness (BeSTOW). The HK police granted him approval to take it. He stayed for eleven weeks in total. We became acquainted during that time and have become good friends since then.

I understand that Gilbert has invited you to Hong Kong before to give talks to the crisis negotiators. Can you tell me about it?

On Gilbert's invitation, I came in May 2013 and 2014. I prepared and presented a workshop to law enforcement crisis negotiators on behaviour-based negotiation tactics, techniques, and procedures. The topics included behavioural threat assessment, instrumental bargaining, suicide intervention, critical incident stress and debriefing, active listening, crisis intervention, and psychopathology.

This is my third visit to Hong Kong, and I am staying from fourth to eleventh November 2018. My days are packed with conferences, workshops, and presentations.

In your view, are there cultural dynamics in Hong Kong that may be different from the United States, and which may impact on crisis negotiation?

The general approach is the same. All people are human, and they have emotions. Suicidal persons are in crisis, but they face the same kind of problems like failed relationships, marriage, and finance. Negotiators use the same tactics. However, the gun culture in the United States makes it extremely different in how we conduct a negotiation. For instance, a person is barricaded in the house or some structure threatening to kill himself/herself or to kill his/her captive with a gun. The gun is always in the picture. Therefore, the subject person has a gun, and the negotiator carries a gun.

The structure of negotiation is that we do not engage in face-to-face talks with the subject person. Typically, we talk with the person over the phone. Not being able to see the face and body language cuts off 80 per cent of the communication. But our specialty is in voice evaluation. That enables us to make judgements on the person's mental state.

In Hong Kong, the majority of suicides are jumping off high-rise buildings. A lot of the time, the crisis negotiator talks to the suicidal person face-to-face. The PNC is therefore good in reading the subject through the face, body posture, and of course the voice.

The US culture is individual-oriented, whereas the Chinese are group-based. In Hong Kong, the PNC adopts a therapeutic approach in dealing with the person who aborts the suicide attempt. They stay a while to comfort the person and reinforce the positive emotions until the ambulance arrives or law enforcement officers take him/her away.

In the United States, the negotiator does his job over the phone. When the person agrees to abort the suicide attempt or to surrender, the negotiator prepares him/her on the steps that will follow. The SWAT team takes the person. The negotiator leaves the scene and almost never sees the face of the subject person at all. It is a low context (US) versus high context (HK) environment.

From my experience of training with the PNC, I think they are doing an amazing job.

I attended your talk at the University of Hong Kong on 5 November 2018. You mentioned that there is often a negotiation within a negotiation. Can you elaborate?

In a US crisis scenario, there are three entities. There is an incident commander, same as in HK; a SWAT team, similar to a tactical team in HK; and a negotiation team. Because of the gun culture, the incident commander, being more action imperative, tends to lean towards the SWAT team to handle the job rather than letting the negotiator handle the subject. Very often the negotiator has to explain the value of the negotiation and assure the incident commander that progress is being made. Therefore, it is a negotiation within a negotiation.

If a suicidal person still killed himself/herself after talking to a negotiator, what message would you give the negotiator?

There is no failed negotiation. They don't fail. The fact that they try to help is all that counts. The subject person makes that final decision. It is not the negotiator's decision, not his responsibility, not his influence.

The crisis negotiators learn this concept in their training, but it is never easy to have to encounter such an experience. That's why peer support is so important. Similar to the practices in the United States, the PNC team conducts debriefing and seeks counselling from the police clinical psychologist, if necessary.

Bibliography

Beautrais AL (2001). Effectiveness of barriers at suicide jumping sites: a case study. *Aust N Z J Psychiatry* 35:557-562. Doi: 10.1080/0004867010060501.

Bennewith O, Nowers M, Gunnell D (2011). Suicidal behaviour and suicide from the Clifton Suspension Bridge, Bristol and surrounding area in the UK: 1994–2003. *Eur J Public Health* 21:204–208. https://doi.org/10.1093/eurpub/ckq092.

Brent DA., Perper JA, Allman C (1987). Alcohol, firearms and suicide among youth. *JAMA* 57:3369–72.

Chen EY, Chan WS, Wong PW, Chan SS, Chan CL, Law, YW, Beh PS, Chan KK, Cheng JW, Yip, PS (2006). Suicide in Hong Kong: a case-control psychological autopsy study. *Psychol Med* 36:815–825. doi: S0033291706007240 [pii] 10.1017/S0033291706007240.

Chen EYH, Chan WSC, Chan SSM, Liu KY, Chan CLW, Wong PWC, Law YW, Yip PSF (2007). A cluster analysis of the circumstances of death in suicides in Hong Kong. *Suicide and Life-Threatening Behavior* 37:576–584. doi: 10.1521/suli.2007.37.5.576.

Chen YY, Gunnell D, Lu TH (2009). Descriptive epidemiological study of sites of suicide jumps in Taipei, Taiwan. *Inj Prev* 15:41–44. doi: 15/1/41 [pii] 10.1136/ip.2008.019794.

Durkheim E (1897/1951) Suicide: A Study in Sociology. New York, NY: The Free Press.

Fisher EP, Constock GW, Monk MA, Sencer DJ (1993). Characteristics of completed suicides: implication of differences among methods. *Suicide and Life-Threatening Behavior* 23:91–100.

Freud S (1957). Contributions to a discussion on suicide. *The Standard Edition of the Complete Psychological Works of Sigmund Freud*, Volume XI (1910). *Five Lectures on Psycho-Analysis, Leonardo da Vinci and Other Works* (pp. 231-232).

Huisman A, van Houwelingen CA, Kerkhof AJ (2010). Psychopathology and suicide method in mental health care. *J Affect Disord* 121:94–99. doi: S0165-0327(09)00230-4 [pii] 10.1016/j.jad.2009.05.024.

Kong Y, Zhang J (2010). Access to farming pesticides and risk for suicide in Chinese rural young people. *Psychiatry Res* 179:217–221. doi: 10.1016/j.psychres.2009.12.005 S0165-1781(09)00488-0 [pii].

Lo SM, Lam, KC, Yuen, KK, Fang, Z (2000). Pre-evacuation behavioral study for the people in high-rise residential buildings under fire situations. *International Journal on Architectural Science* 1:143–152.

Marzuk PM, Leon AC, Tardiff K, Morgan EB, Stajic M, Mann JJ (1992). The effect of access to lethal methods of injury on suicide rates. *Archives of General Psychiatry* 49:451–458.

Reisch T, Schuster U, Michel K (2006). Suicide prevention on bridges in Switzerland. *Psychiatry Danub* 18 Suppl 1:145.

Reisch T, Schuster U, Michel K (2008). Suicide by jumping from bridges and other heights: social and diagnostic factors.

Psychiatry Res 161:97–104. doi: S0165-1781(07)00208-9 [pii] 10.1016/j.psychres.2007.06.028.

Wong PW, Cheung DY, Conner KR, Conwell Y, Yip PS (2010). Gambling and completed suicide in Hong Kong: a review of coroner court files. *Prim Care Companion J Clin Psychiatry* 12 (6). doi: 10.4088/PCC.09m00932blu PCC.09m00932 [pii].

Vecchi GM, Wong GKH, Wong PWC, Markey MA (2019). Negotiating in the skies of Hong Kong: the efficacy of the behavioral influence stairway model (BISM) in suicidal crisis situations. *Aggression and Violent Behaviour: A Review Journal* 48:230–239.

Yip PS, Caine E, Yousuf S, Chang SS, Wu KC, Chen YY (2012). Means restriction for suicide prevention. *Lancet* 379:2393–2399. doi: 10.1016/S0140-6736(12)60521-2 S0140-6736(12)60521-2 [pii].

References

Highways Department, the Government of the Hong Kong Special Administrative Region (2021 May 31). *Ting Kau Bridge and Approach Viaduct*. Retrieved 2021 July 22. https://www. hyd.gov.hk/en/publications_and_publicity/publications/hyd_ factsheets/doc/e_Ting_Kau_Bridge.pdf.

Hong Kong Housing Authority (2021 June 28). *Home Ownership*. Retrieved 22 July 2021. https://www.housingauthority.gov.hk/ en/home-ownership/index.html.

The Newspaper of the Hong Kong Police Force, Off Beat Issue no. 1100 (2017 November 22). *Officers join PNC after taking Crisis Negotiation Course*. Retrieved 2021 July 21. https://www. police.gov.hk/offbeat/1100/eng/6039.html.

The Newspaper of the Hong Kong Police Force, Off Beat Issue no. 960 (2012 February 8). *PNC delegation attends INWG Annual Conference*. Retrieved 2021 July 21. https://www.police.gov.hk/ offbeat/960/eng/.

South China Morning Post (2004 February 26) *Double Life Sentence for Killer of Schoolgirls*. Retrieved 2021 July 22. https:// www.scmp.com/article/445982/double-life-sentence-killer -schoolgirls.

South China Morning Post (2004 December 24) *Hijack Drama Mystery Man in Diplomatic Limbo*. Retrieved 2021 July 22.

https://www.scmp.com/article/483257/hijack-drama-mystery-man-diplomatic-limbo.

Transport Security International (TSI) (2018 June 23). *The Legacy of the 'Miss Macao' Hijack: 70 Years On.* Retrieved 2021 July 22. https://www.tsi-mag.com/the-legacy-of-the-miss-macao-hijack-70-years.

Wikipedia (2021January 29) Home Ownership Scheme. Retrieved 2021 July 22. https://en.wikipedia.org/wiki/Home_Ownership_Scheme.

About the Authors

As police officers, Connie Lee Hamlin and Gilbert Wong had divergent career paths, but both shared the same passion and empathy for police work.

In 1983 Connie joined the Hong Kong Immigration Department as an assistant immigration officer, but, after a number of years, realising that her life needed to make a greater contribution to the community, she decided to apply to the Hong Kong Police Force (HKPF). Over a career spanning twenty-nine years' dedicated service, Connie devoted herself to serving others and her colleagues: working in uniform branch, criminal investigations, criminal intelligence units, as well as service quality, staff training and staff relations branches of the Force. From these diverse duties, Connie earned a wealth of empathetic, communication and decision making skills. From humble beginnings, but with the passion of a life-long learner, Connie earned her master's in social science from the University of Hong Kong in 1995. Nevertheless, Connie's passion for learning and actualising herself never stopped; she had always wanted to be a writer which led to this book.

Dr Gilbert WONG joined the then Royal Hong Kong Police Force as an inspector in 1993 and was promoted to chief superintendent in February 2017. He completed his PhD in behavioural science in the USA, and holds two master's degrees in administrative leadership and counselling from Australia, a bachelor's degree in behavioural science and physiology from Sydney,

Australia, as well as two graduate certificates in education and criminal justice from the USA. He is also a graduate of the world renowned Federal Bureau of Investigation (FBI) National Academy based in Quantico, Virginia, USA and the Harvard programme on negotiation.

Gilbert was first exposed to the world of crisis negotiation when he joined the Hong Kong Police Negotiation Cadre (PNC) in 1999 and was the commanding officer of the PNC between January 2010 and December 2021. Over his time with the cadre, often as the Force's lead delegate to the international negotiator's working group, he has shared his extensive negotiator's experience at conferences in the Netherlands (2004), Germany (2006), Hong Kong (2007), London (2010), Singapore (2011), Paris (2012), Sydney (2013), Scotland (2014), Dubai (2015), Copenhagen (2016) and Belgian (2018).

In 2008, Gilbert was also one of the keynote speakers at the Texas Association of Hostage Negotiators Conference in Texas, USA; in 2011 at the California Association of Hostage Negotiators Conference in San Diego, USA; in 2015 at the Singapore Police Force Resilience Building Seminar; and, in 2016 at the Asian Conference of Criminal & Operations Psychology. Gilbert was also chosen to become a member of the directing staff of the Scottish National Negotiators Course that was held in 2018.

Upon his retirement from the HKPF in December 2021, Gilbert was appointed as a life honorary consultant, Police Negotiation Cadre; an honorary consultant of the Police Carelinks Cadre and an honorary Hong Kong Police college advisor.

In addition to his law enforcement commitments, Gilbert has been a certified clinical hypnotherapist since 2005 and a life member of International Society for Investigative and Forensic Hypnosis since 2011. He was certified as a master hypnotherapy trainer by both the International Medical and Dental

Hypnotherapy Association and the International Association of Counsellors and Therapists in 2012.

Gilbert is passionate about all aspects of life: he is a rescue scuba diver and has so far completed one full marathon and six half marathons. He is especially passionate in understanding the mindset of people he comes across and identifies himself to be a life adventurer, peace maker, fear buster, conflict mediator and relationship builder.

How did the pair come together to be co-authors for this book? As Connie tells it, in 2016, Gilbert, in his capacity as commanding officer of the PNC, was one of the guest speakers in an in-house training course that Connie attended. He introduced the concept of active listening to the group and after a few remarks, Gilbert dived straight in and said, 'Everyone, please gather round this table. Now, try to persuade me to get up.' Without saying anything further, he lay on a desk, folded his arms on his chest and closed his eyes. What happened next? Well, to explain that would have required another chapter in this book, but to keep a long story short, Connie was deeply impressed with Gilbert's lecture, in particular, the case sharing of a crisis negotiation scenario.

Upon retirement, Connie felt even more strongly the calling to pursue her dream in the craft of writing. At the end of 2017, she took a 'Writing Life Stories' short course offered by the Hong Kong University School of Professional and Continuing Education (HKU SPACE). One of the assignments was on writing memoirs and Gilbert came into her thoughts. *Well, I am retired, I have nothing to lose even if he rejects my proposal,* Connie mused. She called Gilbert's office, introduced herself and stated the purpose of her call. A few days later, Connie arrived at Gilbert's office and he shared with her two incidents he had handled as a police crisis negotiator. Connie wrote the stories based on those true incidents from the perspectives of the police crisis negotiators. She mesmerised her class with the stories and easily completed the course.

For Gilbert, this collaboration presented a golden opportunity as he had always wished to look for someone to write a book about the meaningful work of the PNC, in particular the steadfast devotion of police crisis negotiators in diffusing crisis and helping distraught people discover a glimmer of light breaking through a window of hope. Gilbert's wish and Connie's dream converged at the perfect moment. Connie offered to take up the challenge, and this book is the result of their fruitful collaboration.

Made in the USA
Coppell, TX
06 October 2022